BENEATH the SPANISH

VICTOR HERNÁNDEZ CRUZ

BENEATH
the SPANISH

COFFEE HOUSE PRESS
Minneapolis
2017

Coffee House Press books are available to the trade through our primary dis-
tributor, Consortium Book Sales & Distribution, cbsd.com or (800) 283-3572.
For personal orders, catalogs, or other information, write to info@coffeehouse
press.org.

Coffee House Press is a nonprofit literary publishing house. Support from pri-
vate foundations, corporate giving programs, government programs, and gener-
ous individuals helps make the publication of our books possible. We gratefully
acknowledge their support in detail in the back of this book.

LIBRARY OF CONGRESS CATALOGING-IN-PUBLICATION DATA

Names: Cruz, Victor Hernández, 1949–, author.
Title: Beneath the Spanish / Victor Hernández Cruz.
Description: Minneapolis : Coffee House Press, [2017]
Identifiers: LCCN 2017000412 | ISBN 9781566894890
Classification: LCC PS3553.R8 A6 2017 | DDC 811/.54—dc23
LC record available at https://lccn.loc.gov/2017000412

Special thanks to Felix Cortes in the preparation of this text.

PRINTED IN THE UNITED STATES OF AMERICA

24 23 22 21 20 19 18 17   1 2 3 4 5 6 7 8

To Rosalie Roman y Tony Figueroa
To our shared migration
And the many cups of cultura and
History we have drunk together.
Abrazos y amor

"Las épocas viejas nunca desaparecen completamente y todas las heridas, aún las más antiguas, manan sangre todavía."

—Octavio Paz, *El Laberinto de la Soledad,* 1950

"Prejudice and partisanship obscure the critical faculty and preclude critical investigation. The results are that falsehoods are accepted and transmitted."

"When a nation has become the victim of a psychological defeat, then that marks the end of a nation."

—Ibn Khaldun, *Al-Muqaddimah,* 1377

"Writing is one of the most ancient forms of prayer. To write is to believe communication is possible . . ."

—Fatima Mernissi, Moroccan social writer and ardent feminist with an Islamic and secular orientation. She passed away in the days when I was completing this book. Peace be upon her soul.

Contents

Proloco

Some of the poems in this volume were discovered in Puerto Rico and others in New York but were elaborated and expanded in the country of Morocco, North Africa, thus below the Gibraltar stretch and the Mediterranean Sea that caresses the coast of Spain, below the pressure of all those flickering Spanish tongues, beside the Arabic and the French sounds—through it all I produce my Americanized English language writings. English settled into my youthful mind below the phonetics of my family Spanish tongue, thus both my languages are stained. Because English is not the local language in my adopted Morocco, my English stands up inside and becomes a private code. I have been outside the continental United States since 1989 when I moved back to Puerto Rico, and now I reside in Morocco with my family. I am saved from or out of the reach of American commercial propaganda. The world is made up of beautiful differences of total inequalities awesome and tormenting. Everything is awkward and beautiful. My mestizo cubist fragmentation floats like a painting through and from the deformity; outside of history, migratory pirates of contraband. I hope my poems are communication between the fragments. In a real sense I am country-less, yet through my mestizo Caribbean culture I become a citizen of the world, through blood and communion I grow identity branches, various, through words, music, and experience, this life is an adventure. I walk with it. Given Puerto Rico's impossibility to become a politically sovereign nation, my true birth nation has no passport; I remain an American continental on loan, at loose, improvising within Latin jazz. These poems are the wonderings of that spirit. I was born in an area of the planet Earth and now I am in another region of the planet. Earth? It should be called Aguatica; there is more water than soil here. What can we do with the depths and horrors of history 'cept to ride them all out like a wave into creativity and dialogue springing into proliferation?

The prose pieces are in the spirit of notes; they throw light upon the poems and are pregnant with personal biography. These poems and prose interludes are in English with occasional Spanish words, which is how my mind works, bilingually, constantly translating pensive Spanish into English and vice versa.

This makes writing for me an act of translation, of the imagination and its linguas, a desgeografication, crumbling shapes like a cubist work patching up continents; we are still in the age of discovery in the constant search of the connections. Concentration is difficult for many people in this age of electronic gadgetry. Open the books up which are made of tree wood, sit down, and read this gathering of fragments, thinking, and dancing history to make lingual bridges of communication.

Victor Hernández Cruz
Kenitra, Morocco, 2016

BENEATH the SPANISH

TUMBADORA
North Africa/Caribbean Nota Pasafu I

A la memoria de Tata Güines

Listening to Tata Güines
Standing on my Salé balcony
Better I am living Tata
The beats along with my heart
Drinking sound digest shapes
Sparkling thought images
Like a deck of cards
Spinning pressed by a thumb/
Tata self-educated which is
Also my case,
He heard the radio in his
Havana Güines barrio,
Listened to the tumba players
On the street, ask questions
He lived the music.
As I read books and rebelled against
Schools,
Words were in books
What I wanted to feel
Was in books
And the Conversations with elders,
The oral voice.
Music was the ether of youth
The background ocean full of dancing fish,
Rhythm collaborated with my brain
Cells bouncing fast scattered images
perceive it now in Tata Güines's solos,
City flying the current with
A tropical river that surrendered

At my feet the past
Shrimps holding up pictures
Of blue wooden houses
With zinc rooftops,
Huge sky blue.
Tata hits the skin
His fingerprints mark
Language in the sky,
Each slap reminds a flower
To blossom in the Congo,
The tumba pitch falls into
Slow drag
When he rubs
Hide scratching out mountain dirt
His nails animal where it roamed
Righteous beating, a whining
Like beg, laborious pain
Birth.

The cabinet is a montage
Of wood-tight animal,
Sealed like leather zapatos
Tata rumbas and I grow shoes
Foot shakes insects off
Goat flesh stretched
Screams colors of tan tinges
How the cow gave milk,
Tata zapatero
Make my zapatillas
Resbalosas upon the loseta
Glittering/
Below on the street two guys Gnawa
Show up
Before vision I had heard

The metal castanets approaching
Dressed Mayan/or Inca
beyond kaleidoscope colors,
They dance the morning
Café to elevate,
Tata's manos weave
colors merge so many Africas
Meet
Open book of Alejo Carpentier
On Cuban music
Immense rhythmic melodious
Till horizon meets historic cotorra
Scribbling sky danzón
My foot wants to danza South
Sahara down
Tata drumming palms upon
Cowhide
Some drums mule skin
Has been said water buffalo,
Goat tumtu sounds make
A fist garden
Floreos crash into
The Gnawa clank.
Dr. Fernando Ortiz
Researched nkongo Bantu-Congolese:
Conga a dance a circle,
Makuta cows charge into
The rhythm
Listen how distance condenses
Throw step and bop head
I am below the Niger River
Scribble Calligraphy on the Sahara sand
Moving down the wind comes
And away blow designs.

My country is rhythm
The only true legislation,
Political status pales with the cadence.
Dance is
The nature of rolling mountains
Running towards the coast
To jump into the water
Government is the clave,
Adal Maldonado took my
Passport photo out of focus
Similar to the nation
But in tune with Mambo
The secret codes upon document
The camera note:
"Accidental products
Of distraction
And forgetfulness
Will make you Mambo again"
The photographer scribbled in
A note twenty years ago
When we were different images
Both
Trying to enfoco Foco it
Becoming enfoco lens out
Focus out of the blur
Enfoco it Que se Foco,
Photography is a squish
In the darkness of the cave
The silence between
Spaces of limestone
Total obscurity
Snaps/What is in the light.

What is Tata doing
Slow finger-popping
The cowhide
Discussing something
With Chano Pozo
Tata was a kid once
Jumped up on Havana stage
Chano there
Put his hands on the
Tumbadora across from
The composer of:
"Ariñañara"
Started to slap it
Um, kaslap—kaslap.
The elder saw him right away
Saw what he heard, the color
Of the flowers sprouting.

As I listen the air Caribbeans
Now late February
In the depth a motion of Spring
Moisture warm waves of flesh
Skin on skin
Tata Güines maestro classic
Ever to tumba the dora
upon the street of forever
Sun beats.   Sabora.

Primer Encuentro entre Dos Mundos

America is a linguistic mistake from its beginning. It comes from Americus Vespucci, but some speculate that it may be the Nicaraguan tribe the "Amerriques," research Jules Marcou, more recently the Caribbean writer Jan Carew, lots of material still to be cut, food for thought. Did Vespucci change the ortografía of his first name to fit closer to Amerriques? Columbus and Vespucci supposedly visited this part of Nicaragua, which was rich with gold. Air of forgery, fraudulent as most history; you have to grow up to decipher the embroidery of the thieves. The first name Americus is masculine, but Martin Waldseemüller, the map-maker, in 1507 chose the feminine orthography: America (a transgender translation) to name the new continent, as all the other continents had female names. And who were these "indios" out of India, the error persists. Cristóbal Colón, Englishly known as Christopher Columbus, was born either somewhere in Spain or, say many, Geneva and made his way to the peninsula, some speculate him Jewish, a good friend of mine, José Sandoval Sanchez, Arabist scholar from Cadiz, Spain, told me once as we walked the streets, callejuelas of the old Medina of Sweka in Rabat, Morocco, that Colón was a Jew from Menorca, that he took off with another Spaniard who was to be his translator who was also Jewish, Luis de Torres, hidden actual name Yosef ben HaLevi HaIvri, born in the somewhere of the Jewish Diaspora that was Spain, perhaps Murcia. The translator spoke Aramaic, Arabic, and Hebrew, Arabic was the intellectual language of medieval Spain, and who knows if elsewhere they would encounter other Arabic-speaking enclaves or one of the lost tribes of Israel. Could the first nonnative words spoken in the New World have been "Salam alaikum" uttered by Luis el traductor as he approached the Taino chief. Columbus had run into King Ferdinand and Isabella la Católica in Granada, Andalucía, when the Arab caliphs were in ceremony with them handing them deeds of the city, they had just been conquered, giving them the keys to the Alhambra palace locale from which the Christians would administer the re-conquest. Into that drama there was el marinero Cristóbal Colón in the crowd, present, scoping the whole of history, mingling with the people, Muslims and Christians. King Ferdinand and Queen Isabella were cousins, no big thing in the Muslim society of Andalucía in those days where this type of pairing was common, rampant, cultivated by the families throughout the region. Listen, the guitar strings pluck the full moon, the fingernail made of seashells, weaving poetry the troubadours they went singing all the way to the doors of Europe, low Bordeaux, poets dressed like Moros (Moors), Troubadour poesía an approximation towards the lady, praises to the feminine, the gift of Andalucía to the world, serious research tells it influenced the first motions of lyric poetry in Europe. Cordoba biggest city in medieval Europe, did it swing 300,000 inhabitants, streets paved, oil lamp-lit lights with fires under benches, breezes caressing casual readers of books lounge upon benches within park garden walkways, flowers, orange trees citrus fragrance afloat. Public baths where perhaps philosophers Ibn Rushd and Maimonides bathed in the public bathhouses steam sauna heat opening pores elongated drifting conversations through systems of possible ideas. Ibn Hazm perused his intuitions, researching his text on love and lovers, *El collar de la Paloma: Tratado sobre el amor y los amantes*, emotions, loves, lives floated the gardens of his thoughts through the city adorned of balcony flowers. Was Colón a lost Cohen-Kohan, all these names covered, hidden through so much obsession with purity of blood spread in a peninsula of turmoil. Did they mean one single Catholic outlook, purity of religion or purity of ethnicity? Blood what means blood. Historian J. H. Elliott hit the nail on the head when he described this mad obsession of Ferdinand and Isabella, a project he described as a "ruthless, ultimately self-destructive quest for an un-attainable purity." King Ferdinand and Isabella la Católica, kissing cousins, went off the limb now that Granada was back under Christian rule, they were determined to bring all creatures in the peninsula to bow to the Catholic cross, thousands were burned at the stake, public barbecue, the Roman spirit, Latin joy of tribal spectacle, lions chewing people to shreds, Latins what gladiator spectacle put people to fight, Romans, Latin's what, pelea, let's go see. People must've been hiding in closets, burning family tree records; even if you become Christian, suspect still you were, you had to do the wipeout, people burning letters, birth certificates, private fires late at night in backyards, taking walks through country roads with bundles, bush fires, erasing identity, destroy all identifying documents, hide who you are, who you had been. Camouflage. Spain went from a more or less place of religious tolerance to fanaticism, as King Ferdinand and his cousin went Catholic gung ho. So who was it that came on the voyages of explorations? Those that had to leave, pursued by the Inquisition. We were discovered not by Spain as such, but by two Kingdoms, Aragon and Castile; a unified Spain was not yet formed. The majority of settlers showed up into the Caribbean place of the first settlements in the new old world, first it was Santo Domingo, named also Hispaniola, consequently San Juan Bautista, renamed later Puerto Rico, Havana, Cuba, aligned next. Cruelty piled upon a plate of custom, masses individuals unaware of the pain of others. To perceive the cruelty inflicted upon others you have to have a sense of imagination, ah the hurt of others.

What was that original afternoon of spread blue sky: fluffs of white cloud, brisa, nakedness, initial encounter, flesh standing next to enclose torsos, apparel, strangers stench funk from medieval Europe, initial impact; they were in a village, a yucayeque in Taino land, for the Spaniards' native hospitality opened up, waving of hands, with tree branches drawing pictures on the dirt earth, more hand waves, an embrace, the strangers were escorted to bohíos, they were well-treated guests for four days and nights, they got back to the mariner Colón waiting back on the ship offshore, pacing back and forth. They spoke nothing of the hospitality but told of observing the gold they beheld shimmering upon bowls of gourds upon a walk to a river. Gold, oro shining, the colonization of America had begun. It was the tip of the Middle Ages, and in those days gold could talk, as today it still does. Oro. Money, pasta, flus. History dances to gold.

Cuban Taino Cacique Meets Spaniard and the Translator

Tobacco clay flute pipe,
smoke rising into blue firmament,
the guaraguao, the Taino
eagle glides in the sky,
A focused eye details colors of chicken
Feathers, its food down bush earth
on path by a bohío,

Vanilla mixes with tobacco smoke
cohoba nose rush
Shaman inhales snuff bone pipe
burps sudden,
calls to other shamans of the
Key door soul
tells them a strange scent
Novo in the air lingers,
not the blue nature of salt which is the sea
a mirror posted toward
the sun,
something here unique,
trance makes him dance,
Maraca shaking his achiote tinge
flesh, the coloring taste for mosquitoes
keep away,
the nostrils eat space
and tropez upon an alien whiff.

Bohiques call for council
with Cacique,
the elder feather resides
In the rectangular large hut of palms
A center with precious mineral

Cemi sculpted rocks,
the middle, centro, above an oval
Hole for the air,
for the incantation to fly to the stars
Ride the turtle above the clouds.
they inform Guanabanex could be some-
thing in the atmosphere,
Across aires of mountains
but the sodium taste,
Warning could be sea creature,
We just want to speak what the cohoba
tells us
could be a beast,
Your majesty, you have been informed
by the seniors of the
guayaba fragrance, the spirit keepers,
know that something comes
from way out the water
vast like big higuera bowl,
I feel the language noise
trapped in impossible syllables
to utter animal breaths
below the Spanish below
the Arawak
the native pala dental my
Jaw releases me: SOUND.

Later huge boat showed up
in the bay
Like a mirage dream,
or is it there,
naked girls swam
out
Andalucians used to the

djellabas and hijabs
of the peninsular Muslim girls,
long dresses upon castellanas,
majas.
Almost fainted at the
sight of naked nalgas,
swimming swift through the water
bushes open to the air,
Shuma-shame not,
but to the natives
if they had bracelets
or seashell earrings
they were dressed,
The body is everybody
anyone is one any
body flesh akin-to skin
Open air
in the humidity
of the humanity
yuca con yucayeye.
Living. Circular Collection.

People in the boats
what are they,
look how they have
metal heads,
already men taking off
some of the apparel
in the hot new air.
What inferno is this?

Columbus sends translator
with sailor
Go make contact,

speak.
Whom where this
go see Kangaskhan
Where going are we?
find path
some people gathered
along the beach staring
At the drama rolling,
smaller boat comes in
two men get out,
The oar navigator stays
Behind starring at nalgas,
natives take the two strangers
in land,
Meet the cacique chief,
a welcome to whatever
it was,
thing that showed up
wood from big water afloat,
from a where gone in time
and space.
Welcome to my hut
they fed them
dance for them,
gave them feathers,
they tasted cassava bread
next morning, pineapple
slices,
walking feet
dancing toes,
a new kind of flamenco
in a circle
with the sun with the moon,
maraca of night

conch seashell of awakening, morning
passing plaza crowd,
Yusuf translator had never heard words
such sounds,
females talking like sweet
songbirds, Asia must be,
China we are
Calcutta must be near,
these are the Indians of legend,
The error persists
still recounts, oye Indio
Benga-desh, ben aca
We are all in the now,
all now we are all,
Eat me so that I can eat you.
no India Indios. Tainola.

This Caribbean nuevo mundo
ingredients found,
my abuela,
India loca,
guitar birth infant out Laud
La'ud out india zither
(Speaking of Indians)
zither/guitar. . . .
We are the spoken boleros,
Our North African stanza,
Iberia de Marcolino pan y vino,
Mediterranean mellow yellow,
Morena Arab eyes and buttocks
Nigerian chocolate the sculpture
Orisha alphabet of the Lucumi,
Caribe becomes.

Here tis' wees
fabrica of rhythms
history of flavors
who are we not?

Taino/Spain, Africa
Standing face to face
Naked we are
Voices of
Humid loud silence.
Cadence
Printing on the tumbadora skin,
Codes.
Dance Formation
Taste.

Santo Domingo/Puerto Rico
New Dance Commences

Just a short ferry hop from Puerto Rico to Santo Domingo. We are the same people, the same native Tainos, the Spaniards, the jumble they were, los Africanos, from Nigeria, Senegal, Mali, deeper Congo, Cameroon, they used them for labor. The Tainos were slaves as well, who started dropping like flies sprayed with TNT, soon after the conquest. The lost natives are hidden within our gestures, eyes, skin tones, our guayaba of eternity, our cigar of smoke. Güiro scratcher and maracas still with the modern salsa sounds. Spanish maladies like measles did them in, immediately they put them to work in the gold mines, which is what the visitors wanted. Slavery was the economy of the whole ancient world, no one got spared from forced labor, work, given food, a cot to sleep, some gong alarm, sound trumpet get 'em up early to move muscle. Most peoples, all regions of the human planet, can say that their ancestors were slaves, from blond regions of Europe, to immense Asian spells, chocolate Africans to auburn-hair eastern Europeans enslaved. In all wars defeat meant the women and girls had to become concubines to the victors. That's the way of the world, the strong prevail. It's the mathematics. If you play with fire you gonna get burn.

Santo Domingo and Puerto Rico islanders have similar cuisine. Similarities in the historical mofongo/Mangú. The yucca which was here with the Tainos, the guayaba originated perhaps in Central America, worked its way through the whole Caribbean, way before the Spaniards showed up. The plantain and the bananas, which more likely originated somewhere in Asia and brought to Africa early, ah sabor, they must've mushed the potassium in African villages already as in Santo Domingo Mangú and Puerto Rican Mofongo, the other islands mush it up as well. The ñame from Nigeria came over along with the plátano to join the yuca to eventually be bathed in Spanish Virgin Olive Oil. Olives from some Mediterranean regions, valleys in Andalusia. Aceituna to taste the color, Olivos partitioned in dream valleys depth of our souls the Havana of nightlife. Tobacco Mafioso charm nights, Chicago thieves blend with

Batista gangsters, Corporations. They are so pretty, the cabaret girls legs high thrown, that famous leg rising of the Caribbean buttocks of universal renown. The Caribbean Habana, San Juan vacation, picture pretty cards while mountain inside belly's hunger hurt, howl, like some animal inside there? Santo Domingo imprisoned by Trujillo for way too long. People lost. Poverty is one thing, but then these mosquitoes too. Sucking upon rusty barbwire, islands of hungry hunger. All the pictures I've seen of the 40s period of the island show men bone-skinny with white panama sombreros and those old pra-pras straw hats. Flaco. Proximity the bone. What a contrast to today, whence so much food, Caribbean grease has joined with American fast food grease, everybody is sick bloated obese diabetic island infirmary, cardíaco sanatorium. The bad habits of the popular merged with American plasticity, generations imprisoned. Fresh air of pineapple-guayaba might instigate awareness to find yourself somewhere in the maze of a tropical spectacular. Other Caribbean countries have more turf for agriculture, but in Puerto Rico local farming has collapsed. Occasionally local gandules on the road, a station wagon parked before you enter a mountain road, jíbaro with straw hat barking, in a box he has the pigeon peas-gandules, some ñames in a burlap sack the size of tree trunks, but each year less and less. Santo Domingo with Trujillo crimes.

El Señor Pedro Mir, poeta nacional, had to jump to Cuba, stayed there over a decade, while Trujillo the magician performed his acts of disappearance; they worked—it was real magic. People did disappear. Not a scent of your underwear could be traced in the hot humid air. The poet Pedro Mir, we should know is the essence of the Caribbean, born of a Cuban father to a Puerto Rican woman in San Pedro de Macorís, Santo Domingo, you cannot get more Caribbean than that, plus how American emerging in the principio of the new world. Hispaniola was the original settlement of the Europeans, if we could call the Spaniards that came here Europeans; for sure we got invaded by two Kingdoms, the Kingdom of Aragon and the Kingdom of Castilla. The peninsula was a cubist painting in formation, the peninsulares not even in full control of their own territory, its culture mestizo, as the Moorish Muslims were still

16

lingering with their higher culture, it was mestizo of language too, the Arabs were in Spain when the language was still adolescent. The Arabic smoked through the Latin: Spanish like a chick popped its head out of the eggshell. It was how those Spaniards were when they despaired into the blue Caribbean Sea. An unformed formation, a in progress. Who knows what fantasies they entertained? A rumor persists through historical texts that one thousand Moras (Moroccan women who came to Puerto Rico with the first wave of the conquistadors) worked as hetemas, house workers, it has given us a substantial blend of Berber and Arabic blood as the years churn. Just look about—where am I, Marrakesh or Caguas? Hispaniola one of the first names before Santo Domingo, place of the newly arrived Hispanos, La Nueva Isabella original name of Santo Domingo capital, in honor of the reigning Queen Isabel of Castilla. Pedro Mir, taking a great wind from Walt Whitman, was at the crossroads of las antillas hispanas when he wrote "Contracanto a Whitman," you cannot be more centered American than that. Santo Domingo the locale of the original city was in a different place across the river, just like the original settlement in Puerto Rico, which was called Caparra; it too jumped to a more ample bay and was baptized Puerto Rico as Juan Ponce de León got poetic: Puerto Rico city in the rich port. Puerto Rico city was on the island of San Juan Bautista, but years later the names were switched. America is a region accustomed to these transformations. Reversions, forgeries, revisions, thieves, swindlers. We have exhausted stretched dismantled exploded the Spanish language. Our Spanish way beyond the peninsular borders accommodates novo flavors for the tongue. It's the language that was and still is on 104th street Spanish Harlem, I recall it was like a disfigured scratch, almost broken record, eating beans in the corner restaurant where now stands a Tex-Mex restaurant. As Latin American nations became independent of Spain, the local pro-Spanish crown bourgeois kept moving to lands where they were still in control, till finally Cuba y Puerto Rico. Cuba mamboed out of its colonial status in the early twentieth century, Puerto Rico, ay, bendito. La cream de la reactionary crap. The last car of the Spanish train, the Spaniards started in the Caribbean and finished where they started as well. The current migratory problem in Santo Domingo is a phobia that has to be put to rest, or to merengue. The current population of Puerto Ricans on the island does not deserve that immense tropical beauty that paints through the length of our immense smallness. Our eyes glide out from mountaintops, flying like Guaraguao falcons; if we didn't love it to possess it, love dissolves and vanishes. In danger we are of becoming a patch of moisture in the Caribbean.

Ay Bandito, Qué Vaina

The earth came out
of a Calabasa
As the word was in it
floating on water
moisture precipitates image,
Qué calor,
so spoken it sang,
heard speaking tree,
as walked dressed
In flesh caoba,
rocks speech at reach,
tune into my bone,
chisel on stone clay notebook,
Cuneiform tablet inside,
The maracas pencil orality
of remembered places,
the night stars,
the hammock, yucayeques
like beehives, a river crab
Came to my feet to talk
with its mouth legs
trembling like castanets.
It told me something
I obey the enchant canto,
a tree go see out there where,
across the water again place.
Tainos were motion,
nomads of the aquatic-foliage,
sun speaking into the guanine
gold upon chest.
Tainos were roam-mantic, nomads
listening to everything spoke,

a turtle gives a lecture
upon its belly, drawn paintings
the history of the sea.
If there is Vaina in Cayacoa
I'll walk water upon
to Caguana,
Magua casaba with guava jelly
Guarionex smoke from clay pipe.
Naguas dancing
my caligrafía grifa
calligraphy,
guayacán knife chisel soft clay,
circle life symbolic energy
combustion, the waves repeat
tongue
Below the navel button
Bacaloa
Huge curves.
Today mi negrita
is half Taina, a portion Roma gypsy,
splinter from Nazarid kingdom moros
con mucho africoco in the tumbao.
The merengue is foreplay
the Christians pass law to ban it,
now Sevillanas
Mangú plátano
the most in mofongo chew.
The islands were factories
to pull out gold, silver
Now empty carcass,
The sun smiling torture
Upon us.
Back in the metropolis
The gold buys new ships

Sail to the Philippines,
Paid for the marble stairs
of Segovia.
Now we just potassium
Plátano
Guava fruits native
vanishing growing
sugar gone
Chewed gum
Juice spent.

Waves of migrations,
Tsunami
Washington Heights
old bajo Manhattan,
nomad blood drifting
the tribal spirit portable
homes,
Taino settlements were
stepping stones, two more
Moons we pick up and go,
the wind is pushing,
It's what speaks chiseled
onto stone,
That's the biblioteca
a line of rocks
motion energy movement,
rippling. A language of Stone Waterfalls.
pushing on rocks eating
'roz con gandules,
desert bichuela candy sweet.
Betances and Hostos
wanted an Antillean Federation,
A necklace of islands

Cuba Santo Domingo Puerto Rico
Antillas hispanas,
If freedom were a dance
We'd all be in paradise
exhausted from so much guayaba
long time ago.
The real wood hits rock:
Ay bendito Puerto Rico
Americans and all going toward
the infierno directo.

Mi qué Vaina.

Atlantis/Mu

Having read Plato back in 1968 in a Berkeley, California, that has totally transformed, it was the age of the hippies, a phenomenon that I observed from the distance of my diddy-bop Latin from Manhattan slick attire. Jefferson Airplane, Bob Dylan, the Mamas and the Papas. The Beatles had already bolted from some other planet called Liverpool. The song "California Dreaming," by then José Feliciano was happy with the lyrics, accompanied my West Coast fantasy. The disease of reading infested me very early, kid around eleven, twelve years old, reading and swollen imagination. One foot in the streets, the other dragging through poetry. In California hung out and achieved cannabis haze blend maintaining a rush and scope of eye for trouble, habit from New York barrios. I had come to live in Berkeley from Spanish Harlem New York. I had been living in the top of a theater called the Gut Theater, run by a Colombian theater enthusiast Enrique Vargas, we had been doing theater in the streets of El Barrio. I had also during those years been involved with a reading tutorial school there in the neighborhood, it was through a program run by Colombia University students. We were high school students teaching younger kids how to read, doing poetry with them, and singing songs. We didn't know what we were doing, we were learning as we went along. Arriving in California young as I was I had already transit through the streets, the Afro-American-Puerto Rican civil rights movements, remember endless rent strike organizations and marches in downtown City Hall. I was mambo fast and California was slow speed for me. Berkeley was full of rock music, which my ear could never get tuned into, but I had brought with me the records of Tito Puente and Eddie Palmieri so that I could stay in tune with the clave of the salsa rhythms, the music of my upbringing in Latin Manhattan. Some years before going west, which was in 1968, I was a youngster flying the streets of the Lower East Side. I started reading early, the language skill came to me with minor effort as if it were already inside and all I had to do was give it a tap to open it, it sailed smoothly through me as inside I was struggling to keep the phonetics of my first language, the Spanish, in practice, atop of which I pasted the English grammar. The two languages bumping into each other. By the sixth grade I was reading way above my level, I was at a high school grade level. I was eating any book that came into my hands. I discovered the Broadway/Fourth Avenue book row stores in the early sixties, which was New York's old book row right there in walking range of my Lower East Side tenement building. There were many stores still in business, books were outside on shelves and tables, paperbacks were something like three for fifty cents. I went to work helping some friends that had jobs in a laundry making deliveries to the Stuyvesant and Peter Cooper middle-class projects and made money from the tips and each day came home with two to three dollars, the next morning up early took an enthusiastic walk toward the west side to Broadway, curiosity smirk across my face as I pranced over to peruse among the shelves of the bookstores. Did I go to one of the original Barnes & Noble bookstores right off Union Square Park? I had heard of some writers from the reading of school literature textbooks, Hemingway, Edgar Allan Poe, other writers some older friends were whispering to me about, also I had made friends with some of the neighborhood beatniks that were living in the tenements alongside the Puerto Ricans, and talking with them and looking at their bookcases I learned of more writers. I gave myself up to discovery, picking up books after reading the first few pages. One of the North American beatniks told me about *The Catcher in the Rye* so I started reading Salinger, also Mark *Huckleberry Finn* Twain in real inexpensive editions that I found thrown around in these big wooden boxes outside the bookstores, the books were put into brown grocery bags like you get at the bodegas, and it was good this way because I didn't want the guys on the corner, my street friends, to know that I was reading books. I was that way, a loner, though I was social and friends with everybody on the block, I was never part of any clique, my friendships were passive, even fleeting, I spent hours reading, thrown on an old sofa that me and a friend of the building took up to the roof, sat there hidden upon the roof of the sky-light staring toward the Empire State and the Chrysler Building, which was momentary scenery as I raised my glance from whatever worlds I was reading about. At first I did not read poetry books that much, poetry was something that I lived. Early on in my house (apartment) my mother's brother Carlos would occasionally recite poems from the oral tradition of Latin America, I remember in particular "El Brindis del Bohemio," it always made me cry. I was affected by language as a kid. Those family recitations and the lyrics of the boleros that my mother listened to, the family sang together, those were my first sense of words as expressive emotion, my introduction to poetry. My early readings were history and narratives; I could not yet reach poetry locked in books as lectura. Taking walks further up Fourth Avenue I ended up at the Jefferson Bookstore across from Union Square Park in my youthful zest for knowledge. Years later I learned that the Jefferson Bookstore was owned by the Communist Party. They would have sale books spread on tables in the fashion of the other Broadway book row stores; it was here that I first purchased the poems of Lorca, the Spanish poet, in English translations, the Turkish poet Nâzim Hikmet, and Pablo Neruda, the Chilean poet who eventually would win the Nobel Prize. I took all these books to the tenement building where my family lived and escaped up to the roof and on top of the world disappeared from reality. My father and mother having divorced some years earlier, I felt totally without structure; it was my father who had a firmness that mother and her family lacked, alone and without direction I escaped into language. I went up to the twelfth grade in high school but never bothered to get my diploma, feeling independent knowledge for me was in the reading of books and in conversations with many different types of people. Making friends with poets and writers, I was already starting to do my thing. New York was a world of turmoil, chaos, many of my street friends had fallen to heroin, I went a lot to the Ortiz Funeral Home on Third Street, to see and mourn dead friends. Street violence was a spontaneous jump that could engulf you when you least expected, the world was collapsing all around me, it sharpened my resolve to escape out of New York. To a place where I could read and write hidden from the humongous animals of the New York streets. Herb Kohl, who I had met in my East Harlem High School days, informed me from Berkeley, California, where he had by then established for himself an opportunity to work with young people doing poetry workshops. Thus upon an evening of 1968 my friend who is really like my cousin by now, David Henderson, the poet, "Mayor of Harlem," gave me a ride to the airport and go west young man, something was calling. A trip that changed my life forever. In Berkeley I stayed first with Herbert Kohl; I remember once walking up the hill to where he lived, my footsteps under a tree disturbed a giant white owl that was in a trance upon a branch, it fluttered its white wings, I can still see those wings so bright. There was so much to see and to know, so much to eat, tela to cut, excited meeting Chicanos/Mexicanos, and over in the Mission District of San Francisco, Salvadorans, Nicaraguans, flavorful Mexican food, the beans were crush-smashed, a familiar flavor to me for I grew up eating pinto beans as well, this refried version was like an accent upon the flavor. On Telegraph Avenue, I met Fred Cody, owner of Cody's Books, met Moe Moskowitz of Moe's Books, who was next door, and spoke much to him about our shared New York. He was a Jewish guy from the city, his accent reminded me of the Lower East Side people I met in the 50s, Moe sitting back at the entrance next to the cash register always smoking his cigar. Books have always saved my days and nights. In New York looking out windows of snowfalls and five below zero outside, hot tenement brick ovens of radiator vapor, my hands holding trees squeezed down to paper, ink words dancing mind mambo. In California long stretches to get anywhere, Cannabis sativa influenced reading of text, sometimes stream of consciousness abrupt halt coming back realizing I had read the same paragraph four times over, get the tempo nailed down and proceed; many books I read in this period I have in recent years had to reread. It was through the shelves of Moe's Books and Shambala Booksellers next door that I became interested in the occult, went loco reading Le Plongeon, John Bennett, Ouspensky, Gurdjieff, from India *The Ramayana,* James Churchward talking about some Mu, who?, continent out in the Pacific now sunken; stumbled upon Plato's *Timaeus and Critias.* Speaking and hanging with Chicano/Mexicano friends I was informed of Aztlán and details of Maya, Azteca esoteric theories; the connections between worlds has always fascinated me, and overall the antiquity of humanity, which is being pushed back in time by recent research. Egypt, where the Greek Solon went to hear about Atlantis from the priests.

What I mostly realize about history, reality, is that there is a veil of mystery that cannot be penetrated exactly as we wish, and it is fine with me that not knowing is a state of mind, knowing that you do not know, it gives in to wonder, mystery, possibilities, imagination.

Bajo Mundo

On the ocean floor
Suspend unspeakable fish,
Purple mountains,
Cavernous avenues
Of psycho sound,
Echoes of plugged ears
Light from below
Another sun,
A warmness of cold gold
Endless space,
Andres Segura, deer dancer
With the Ballet Folklórico
Of Mexico spoke and resounded
That the Mechica Aztecas
Claimed origin in another
Constellation: Andromeda.
As Aztland was a star in it.

Andromeda dancing illumination
Sky fire
Ptolemy saw her being
Chased by a sea dragon
Deep in the northern
Shadows of vast sky,
I saw her once in the Bronx
Brook Avenue walking
Toward Teatro Puerto Rico
With her blue kankanas,
Spring day of her
North African curves,
Eyes moons on the coast
Mediterranean disappearance,

Where are these places?
Myth in gone,
A Paradise, a heaven,
La Gloria,
Original home?
Now clamoring from this squalor
To go somewhere else and
Become eternal sensation,
Your body finalized in some
Box/blanket buried tierra earth,
Will you be ether changing colors
Like a rainbow or rolling in music
Bebop Lester Young,
Phraseology of Stan Getz,
Pulses of
Puente/Tito Rodríguez's of mambo/
I just moment the breath,
This instant corazón,
Whatever was and now isn't
Perhaps will be again
We myth the future
Endless repetition,
The clave of the son montuno
Is a circle,
Infinity of rhythmic patterns,
Somewhere you are
A coco in the atmospheric
Horizon.
The Navaho are in the
Patterns of the Berber rugs,
The Hopi in the geometry
Of the arabesque balcony
Spirals, circles, infinite
The sun's hip points

Like the female she is
To circle turquoise feathers,
Bright realization that the world
Has been shuffled around
Like dominoes upon a table,
Under the Iceland
Hard water ice sheets
Lizards immortalized in minerals,
The once tropic night
Danced to the south,
Rose as Caribbean Volcanic
Tips, thus if walking I am
Upon the remnants of Atlas's
Turf, Atlantic Aztlán,
Birds chirping morning
Could be ancestors,
Sense Plato the years'
Passage seems more
Like philosophy or spirit
Than land broken, sunken,
Somewhere, Thera, Sardinia
Tsunami, the Pillars of Hercules
Combustion somewhere,
Plato approves perhaps
Through Egyptian encounters
The craftsman who elaborated
The existent universe,
Not chance
Well-administered dance
Rumbero calligraphy determines floor.
"Mu" sign of James Churchward
Reading too many books
Speculative interest of symbols
Chiseled into stone.

The brilliance of the Pacific
Is that India is there
India is enough obscurity,
Mysterium
Probing for a lifetime.
Azhlantis root word of Nahuatl
Origin
Island upon lake
The moon man in the water,
Azhland of heron white
Tint, islet of egrets,
Place of white light feathers,
Huitzilopochtli came to
His people singing like
A hummingbird, Colibrí
Listen to the song
They followed,
His mother the woman with
The serpent skirt taught
Him how to sing,
They followed to Tenochtitlan
Today Mexico City
Saw there an eagle swallow
A serpent atop boulder
Lakes there
Travel the Mechicas out of
Azhlantis to now where
Not sunken not of this earth
Atlantis, the priest told
Solon about the subconscious,
That's what was sunken
About unseen spirit motion,
Reincarnation
You recycle the ages

Shifting, like Buddha in
His mantra under a tree
Of many befores.
Atlantis and Mu
Will not be found below water,
Submerged in caves,
Azhlantis will fall upon
Us from the sky, like rain
Of roses and white lilas
With a blue cielo of serpent
Waving,
Marriage of the brujas
Or drop from beaks of birds.
Canta. Arrives the summer
Sky blue
The road from Cidra
To Aibonito
Mountain green waves
Atlantis visuales there appear
Eyes in guaraguao sky glide.
What other plato in paradise
Of Atlantean fish,
What other who, Mu Who
Who what
Where?

Hispano Caribbean/America Latin

"Cuando en la historia de un pueblo se advierte la ausencia o escasez de ciertos fenómenos típicos, puede asegurarse que es un pueblo enfermo, decadente, desvitalizado. Un pueblo que no puede elegir entre varios estilos de vida: o vive conforme al suyo o no vive."

—*José Ortega y Gasset (España Invertebrada, 1964)*

(My country was a dream of childhood.)

Whatever it was, or was it? Where were those places, were they here, how time changes space. Where I was born was Aguas Buenas, circa 1949, fin del mundo, born in the house by comadrona (midwife), singsong throwing plants, leaves Taina smoking cigar Doña Lola, all the houses in the barrio made of wood, painted blue, orange, yellow, the street like a hill slant climbing toward heaven. Did Miro paint our street? It was pre-industrial; I learned how to go to the bathroom upon a latrine. Stand in front of the house, view of green mountains, ovals in the tropical sky wind blue or gris immediately, cloudy, rain. Rain. Such is the tropical climate. A rain factory, morning heat raises moisture, clouds gather for afternoon showers. The Caribbean is an aquatic drizzling world, rains profusely, ever read *One Hundred Years of Solitude,* Márquez tells us it rained for four years and eleven days, rain and war the background of Macondo, water like sea waves down the streets, best to be an amphibious reptile. But we humans. There we were in the middle of the Caribbean living our traditional village life, we were once indigenous, once Spaniards, we were the Africans brought here to work, cultivate agriculture, mix the cement, make the bricks, build Old San Juan, a medieval walled city. When I was a child boy I accompanied my mother and my grand-mother going down to the river where all the women went to wash clothes upon the banks, banging with slaps of wood upon rocks the clothes, the songs, the gossip, chirping women of long dresses. River this time crystal-clear clean water. Bamboos leaning in waves stooping as if drunk. Where is that river now, I can't really find it, along the path of what was once a river they have built a baseball league, channeled the river below ground, under big parking lot the current, so it is hard now to decipher the landscape of the past, that spot, where is the place that was vibrant currency? The streets of my boyhood town not yet paved became muddy when it rained, which was always the case. It's still the same rainy region; it always rains at three in the afternoon as if to chase the school kids back home.

The Tainos, the Spanish, the Africans created a fusion culture, they became a soup. We are no longer in the native bohíos, the palm frond native homes which still lined the mountains in the 30s, 40s, 50s; they made it into the 60s some old-timers have told me. Childhood through the barrio streets, my legs spread over square latrine box of cement, the caca abyss below, make sure do not slip. I got to change bottles for pirulí lollipop cherry red licks, shorts running wind warm. Black boots I recall of my running childhood feet. The wooden houses, Rafael Hernández boleros, melody in front of my eyes, cement trucks tilted upon the street which slants down toward the plaza. Everything was being covered with cement. The wooden boards of the houses permitted slices of wind breezes to penetrate; listen to the squabble of the chickens under the house, any conversation that passed in the street was in your ear. I suppose we proceeded into progress; people just said they were exiled from el campo, the dirt streets paved, tar smell funk, seemingly a new phase of less goats, horses, oxen, cows, burros through the main street. Street named Muñoz Rivera, father of the primero elected governor, this hijo who was poised in a white suit somewhere simultaneous with my childhood, must've been sitting in a big house still a lo español. In that chaos of social history, upheaval of change, I was a boy running with black boots and dark blue shorts. In the the plaza where I heard voices coming from a subterranean level, Manolo, some guy I heard speak, never saw him but he was always a plaza companion, across the alcaldía; another corner the casino club for dancing, always the Catholic Church and the bank adjacent plazas, another building structure full of tobacco leaves, where mother and abuela worked in the tobacco chain, splicing leaves, taking the stem out from the center, preparing the plant for the tobacconist to roll into cigars. It was Aguas Buenas, Comerío, Aibonito of the times. Saw families jumping into station wagons, the big people saying they going to Nuyol, a place not this place, somewhere you went on something called an avión, through the sky through the clouds. We too finally got to jump on one of those metallic birds. We made it to the Lower East Side where something called a building confronted us. Behold the tenements, no mountains to be seen. We left Latin America and came to the developed city of New York. We arrived from another age, another culture, another language, another landscape. Where are we, I asked myself, as the English pushed through the cold of the years new syllables fresh dissolving within the saliva of my Spanish-flavored tongue?

"Dicen que en la distancia es el olvido."

Childhood in the Latin Caribbean

I was child mountain
lived in a Latin American country
till I was five,
My grandfather was a cigar maker,
a tobacconist, rolled the leaves
Ancient craft.
Mother and father brought
together by custom routine,
young and curious,
primero balcony stares,
held hands for a while.
The plaza, Catholic Church,
life there was Pueblo ocio
arrested by boredom
Rutina tedium.

Marry young jíbara
wooden house
Christ on the cross
over the bed
Covered by mosquito net,
nocturnal bolero voices
could be Julio, el Bohemio
in canción
Grandfather/Abuelo
always sang,
everyone cantando
Even the rocks sang.
I was there in the air
not yet born but alive
counting the tamarindo
Coconut lollipops.

anxious to be white sombrero
getting hints upon the weaving of straws
glances from eyes like music
Shadow depth, the porcelain tinge
Surrounds the pearl black eyes
Of the girls.
Otro lelolay.

Destiny had other plans.
Life has no pity,
It moves forward.
Someone told me
man of father's generation that
he was quiet in school,
that he made it somehow
from mountaintop barrio Bayamoncito
into the town each day
the tribulation labor, secret that
people took in silence,
my mother refunfuñar (bickered)
as her family was everyday town-
people,
her father the dignity of the
tabaqueros,
black café and brandy six in
the morning rolling cigars,
sun falling singing with Alegría boleros
Together rolling the life given,
the tobacco cape leaf
Wrapping the guts, pajilla
tight cigars.
Later Chicago Mafiosos will smoke
them
Porto Rico American Tobacco Company

New Jersey 'mericans
owned the production of cigars
los tabaqueros just rolled
what the mountains gave,
the Taino ancestral leaf
in your fingers,
To which they sang
Poetry of the Spanish golden
Age in Cuban bolero sway.
Habaneros for the New York
bankers,
Antiquity awakes in the
now, the past dreams in the future.
Boleros de Rosa-Julia
Persist, the image tomorrow
somewhere
Someone else the same,
a different similarity,
my root of earth.
Modernity does what it does?
I maintain
macho Cimarrón,
the old café tobacco cane night
Flavor churning
grind bones.
Limbes tamarindo, coco
at Doña Rufa's.
Café con leche,
ensalat bacalao
Rosada beans,
yuca with olive oil
twas my country,
Black eyes
launch from black hair

Skin rosa brown,
What can improve?
Evolve?
upon a day
of our hot wintertime,
We jumped from the
Fire
Into the freezer
Cold November,
The cruelest month
Excusez moi
T. S. Eliot
April lluvia
Brings Mayo flores.

Mother's schooling
included math riddles
With poetry jingles,
As father Severo accomplished
numbers in addition
astute with the economy
he never slept.
Forward we went into
New York of the early
50s into the future
with the past,
into the English
with the Spanish,
in a movie rerun
the mountains melt
with the bricks.
Eyes hang sideways
upon guayaba trees frozen
East side school yards,

Guitars strum history
bolero broadcast
amor trovadores,
singing back into the layla night
the lyrics.
Awkward language sounds
Still photos crumbled
In compost moisture.
A lone plaza photograph
A post spelling RECUERDOS
Of a country of childhood
Which dissolves
bright memory,
As
Now a now, is all there is.

San Agustín/Florida

The eastern south of the continental United States could have been another Latin American country, originating in San Agustín, Florida, in 1565, under Spanish rule, and still a municipality today, oldest of the mainland USA cities.

What did the natives call the homeland to describe its beauty: florid seaside, green carpet underfoot, ocean vistas, rivers and ponds of cold-blooded reptiles, descendants of dinosaurs, basking in the Everglades? Smelling funky in Puerto Rico, Juan Ponce de León got an itch, intuition of more turf to steal and rumor of gold and fountains of youth, and took flight north. It was early in 1513. The adventure became misadventure that led to his finale, as eventually a poison-tipped arrow pierced his nalga tissues and nerves to taste blood. The Spaniards pulled back. The crazy natives didn't want to be told what to do, didn't want to work. Back in Cuba, the native chemical weapon did its work for Ponce de León's demise.

The British pilgrims and Dutch merchants and investors were nowhere on the horizon when the medieval gates of San Juan were erected. They were still over a hundred years away. Santo Domingo and San Juan would become cities with cobblestone streets and callejuelas, horse-drawn carriages, plazas, plazuelas, patios, and balconies in the Andalusian style, wine bars/cavas, bibliotecas with books growing yellow in the humid and salty Caribbean air. Workers atop scaffolds building the San José Church. Sir Francis Drake tried to take the Island—and the French and the Dutch as well as the British. They all failed.

Tampa has always been a cigar-making center, like much of Cuba. Florida could have been part of Cuba. José Martí raised funds for the Cuban independence struggle there. The Anglos' Fort Marion, where resistance fighters of the "Indian wars" were imprisoned in 1872, was actually the sixteenth-century San Marcos Spanish fortress. San Agustín was a center for runaway slaves from the American South, bottom tip of the railroad to freedom. In 1693 the Spanish government gave these Africans and their descendants their freedom, and Fort Mose (Gracia Real de Santa Teresa de Mose), just north of San Agustín, would become the first free Black town in North America. Oh, yes, Afros had to convert to Catholicism, as the Inquisition thrived; the Spanish kept "their" slaves elsewhere. The first African-American child born in continental USA was born there in that Latin region past, where Martin Luther King Jr. would talk and organize in the modern freedom movement. So, in a way, the civil rights movement had seeds in this neo-Latin enclave.

Florida, Latin center at the start (and today), the beginning and the end of the Caribbean. Imagine, there actually was a Treaty of Paris (1763) that gave Florida to the British, a history fact insane enough to seem incredible. San Agustín is a barrio in Habana too. So, Ponce de León and his fantasy entourage interrupt the Seminole people and the crocodiles—must've been a case of spook sees spook. No Hollywood creation can ever reproduce it. Later, Africans enslaved in nearby Georgia took to disappearing and finding the Seminole enclaves (the name itself, Seminole, from Spanish cimarrón, "runaway slave"), becoming one with the families, jumping into the powwow circle, their language fusing with their hosts' to produce the Afro-Seminole Creole. Perhaps these Africans and their children contemplated the sea from there and dreamt of swimming back home to Africa. Today, Florida might as well be a Latin American country. The air is Spanish; dishes of plátanos and arroz moro for lunch; everywhere, café, cubanito, negrito, azuquita pa' ti San Agustín, St. Augustine—first European settlement in North America. What are the Americans talking about when they say "immigrants"?

More Nuevo Mundo

"I ran away from the Hispanos
on a boat,
Chasing a perfume hint toward the North
of nowhere,
a fragrance which was almost
A sound."
Ponce de León left his big
house in Caparra,
White walls, Arabesque tiles,
island of San Juan Bautista
a bay
From which he sailed off,
who were these explorers?

Who were once open mouthed
gasping at Moorish Cordoba,
Roman Hispanos
wrapped in Muslim mantas
warm in the merging Spanish,
tango of Latin and Arabic.
Wood upon the ocean waters
ships, ears and noses inflated
by the winds, canvas flapping sails
Percussion, wide latitude whatever
the mother sends,
hijos de puts
who the Vandals conquered
Moros swift submission
identity blossom,
Fragrance of citrus with roses.
the conquered conquer on.

A child in a tantrum
mar Abierto
Va'paya
going to where
to be somewhere
No one
to be someone.
History is made
by so many nobodys,
So many of them
they have crusted
At the edges of a pie,
tanto loco que hacen
orilla,
Of the lions there is de León
roaring beyond his stature,
the Tainos were the Jews to his
Hitler claws,
was de León derailed to the Bahamas,
puzzled in the islands
They all look the same,
naked pickings,
Some were actually empty
of human population: birds
and reptiles of nervous
icy blood
"el mundo es ancho y ajeno"
Thank you, Ciro Alegría.
in that alien new north the Spanish
set down the grid for St. Augustine
Old pattern in virgin turf,
the Seminole somewhere distant
Teepees secret Creek lineage,
the Spanish kept at distance,

not welcomed
enough many became cadavers,
The Seminole were never conquered
not by the Spanish not by the
Anglos.
California once part of
Mexico,
The USA kept invading land
As now it searches for oil
Lands Middle East.

The first flavor of the
continental Estados Unidos
was this Seminole/Creek
enter the Spanish-Latins,
when the Saxons, bored in the
Suburbs of London,
the Dutch in the cold
canals of Amsterdam,
did they all smell luz
warm light of the sun.
We must know that it was,
the pull of the sea,
the Spanish looking to find Asian
spices
bolted out of boorish Castilian
prairies pampas stretch of savannahs.

Spanish the first
Euro nonnative language here,
speak well, when you text the book,
Latinos the original pilgrims,
the mix would have been
Caribbean/Brazil Racial stew

not
The sharp white/black divide
of Anglo north,
Color would have been most fuzzy,
blurry, jagged shades of tones.
Ah yet Augustine is
the Caribbean
The Seminole mouth
tasting the black beans
The plaza in Tampa
like the plaza in Comerío
Tobacco just as well.
St. Augustine original ciudad
of the USA
New Cordoba Continental
the grid of the street/
Architecture created in moro Spain,
"America! America! God shed
his grace on thee"
teach Children in the schools
How magic true reality is
marvelous
practical everyday
If you go through
the weaving pulling strings,
Cloth algodón of colors,
History is imagination
It all has happened
In the future
Coming up chocolate Elixir
The arrows are words
To Free the imagination
of the truth.

What Is the Lower East Side

The lower tip of Manhattan, the ass of the island, el culo de la isla, a piece of rock surrounded by rivers, the Atlantic not far. Historians say that the Dutch purchased Manhattan for the equivalent of sixty guilders, whatever that was in dollars, but wait they gave it in trinkets, pots, beads, etc., what money natives need for in the world they lived, qué, for what, to go to Chase Manhattan to make a deposit? It was a custom of all native peoples to give gifts one to each other, especially when they were in transit through the land of others, space not familiar to them, and this was the spirit of the Munsee, Canarsi Indios, selling land was a concept not comprehended, couldn't even be thought of that such such was possible, they were exchanging gifts as was their always manner-custom. It was just another day of social communication. Then just go on their way. Manhattan when it is summer is semitropical bliss, imagine back then, green, clean clear rivers and streams, animals roaming, hopping about, hills mountains flowers the warm air full of bees, ladybugs, birds singing, canoas floating stream down the East River, Hudson, visual bays bright like Gauguin paintings caressed the rock-littered banks, fried fish served with berries as spring flowers wind serenade. Indigenous people had no concept of selling the earth; what other films have been invented to cover the theft. James Delancey (one of the Delanceys, as all the males in the family were called James) had a farm that was a good piece of the Lower East Side. Delancey was a landmark street for the Loisaida neighborhood that I knew, this area or right below it was once known as Corlear's Hook, fecund with putas and thieves. Wino Bowery fame memories pop like cartoons, original Popeye and Donald Duck, Porky Pig, "what's up folks" walking in the cold breeze south down Avenue B turn at that cuchifritos restaurant on the corner the window full of fatback, fried fritters, plantains like the island of Puerto Rico, next was Barneys Boys Town, the adolescent apparel store where I once purchased a leather coat. Turn of the century, further down, this was Irish jumping, Italian spaghetti barrio The Five Points area. Originally it was a lake, beautiful within Manhattan summer, when it was all those hills green and abundant of berries, cherries, breezes bouncing off the clean pristine East and Hudson Rivers, Manhattan without buildings. With progress the air now flows stinky of bricks, cement, steel, industrial fumes, glass windows, automobile exhaust suffocates, disfigures the air, asphalt of hurried stress. This lake dried became the sight of the Five Points called the Collect. Coincidence but in Puerto Rico's Santurce area there was a shantytown barrio on the water, the bahía, which was known as La Colectora; it got full of jíbaros migrating from the agricultural countryside to get closer to the Metropolitan area menial jobs, lumps of shit floating in water all around the residents. The Five Points slum, the original American ghetto. The Irish mixed with freshly freed African slaves, Italians, Catholics foreign to Protestant America. That particular reality, Irish Italian and African American mixture, it was an everyday fusion of living, working out by the docks, heavy loads, bars to drink shellac, the exhaustion, brothels to take care of what ails you. Here was a barrio of Germans, Irish, Chinamen, Italians, free blacks, working people struggling to put food on the table for families. The Irish and the Afros saloon'd, boogaloo'd together, creating friendships, relations, marriages, children. Master Juba was there, cream de caramel-looking young man feeling the Irish dancing with their jump, adding his African timing, came out tap dancing, a very early expression of that art form that later African Americans continued to perfect, foot wizards, magic toes. The immigrant neighborhood par excellence. The place from which the Gershwin brothers Americanized. I got a glimpse of that Jewish-Euro immigrant barrio in the midfifties. That was a Lower East Side world now lost forever.

Lower East Side Red Brick Blues

Soda pop one hand
pizza the other.
Mulberry Street my foot,
I walk around
make sure buildings don't
fall upon head,
edifices built for the
Workers old and tired,
big families no fit,
antiquity of bricks, cement
talking Yiddish, slant Irish,
Eyetalian.
steps, stoops, hard
Buttock observatory
street drama.
Tenement stairs groan
step marble a cold
Mineral moan,
iron wrought banister design,
meaning lost.
Beauty at first,
When I saw the building
first days of my own migration
into the metropolis
long view tunnel upward
there skylight dispersed silver light,
top roof floor a room,
Down through the marble stairs,
hallway little tile squares,
Brass door entrance handle knob
along with the brass mailboxes
shining still then

Sight beauty in my youth,
bonito shiny glaze
stare eye see veneer art delight.
close my eyes now it all comes
back.
Eternal.

The super, Charly, this Russian
Jewish old-timer
Told me
"was lotta gambling round here
Gambling sonabitches no good
Irish sonabitches no good
German sonabitches no good
Jewish sonabitches no good"
Like what he told me of
the Old lowlife,
Poricans he called
The Spanish
"sonabitches no good"
For Charly everybody sonabitches
no good.
Deep Lower East Side
now Chinatown
parts of Italy petite
brushing up against what
Municipal courts and business districts
were in times past
the Five Points slum ghetto,
pretty Molly McCollum
blue eyes in desire
want of attention,
She can shake her buns,

a beer or two,
the Tavern of forgetfulness.
Eerie gutter Street,
cut faces of red dark yellow
eyes, men on the conner,
staring stabs of knives from start
jump no salute
working slave class squirm
spit insults stacked like layers
of hate against the heart.
America apart from me this cáliz
cup of foul occupation.
It is better to be slapped in the
face
than to have the humanity of
Five Points shellacking you ass
with fire tongues on blast.
Al Capone sharpened his wits
upon its gutters,
Gambling holes
who protected them.
Italian, Irish cojones,
closest thing to a smile
was a smirk from a frown face,
Mope glances.

Today you worry about the South of Bronx
That is Mickey Mouse cartoon,
Bomb out burned down,
The Five Points looked that way
Every day,
After the Draft Riots Five Points
looked like Hiroshima

after the atom bomb.
It had nothing else to do
except disappear.

Pockets of Irish families
were amongst the Puerto Ricans
Of my instance,
On 11th Street that beautiful girl
Arlene, her sister Katherine,
mother, uncle with red beer face,
drank with the PoRicans,
the girls fell in with Rican guys
all Catholics,
Irish-Rican kids running around.
Freckles sprinkled upon brown skin.

The Lower East Side,
el culo de Manhattan,
saw myself in a sway hammock
reading Henry Roth's
Call It Sleep
the Avon books paperback
With the photo of fire escapes
clotheslines backyards
Such reality to my dreams
Recurrence of.
Tenements like painting hues
Corner streets of red brick blues.
I was awake within the
Nightmare.
(A sangre fría)
That too.

New Orleans y Todo Ese Jazz

Jazz is a criollo music from the Latin Caribbean. New Orleans is a Caribbean City Latin American, aligned to the Caribe islands, Latin America, France, Spain, and the rest of the world more so than any Protestant northern region. Close to Mexico, Latin-African Criollo mix like the Caribbean islands, what wonder jazz fusion is but this melt. The Cabildos, African religious organizations in Cuba, maintained authentic African rhythms and culture alive in Cuban society to an extent not heard of in the northern African slave centers, the only northern place that Afros were able to keep their drums was New Orleans, Louisiana. Another factor which made the Caribbean accommodating to African cultures was the proximity in climatic realities between el Caribe and parts of Africa like Nigeria and the Congo, the similarities in tropical flora; the Tainos were still about during the early stages of African slavery and the wise made correspondence. The dance in the Areyto round, the Africans joined right in. The invocation of spirit began to blend, melt, as the popular people talked to each other, and Spanish has never been the same, it became something more open to vocabulary of new fruits and cuisines. A timing, a tempo out of the fusion. When the port city of New Orleans was under Spanish rule we were all under the same umbrella, Mexico, Puerto Rico, Cuba, the same Spaniards, as such the Spaniards exchanged military marching bands, musicians, way back before the Jazz Age. Jazz is Blues and Gospel. Homegrown by African slaves, a blues and gospel that came right along with the bursting of the chains. A nativity in place. Could an aspect of its rhythmic pulse have been within the whisperings of the Danzón, the Habanera rhythms of Cuba, the Danzón spread like fire to Mexico's Yucatán, Vera Cruz region, eventually to New Orleans. Many Mexican musicians could be found among the bands that were marching in the Saints. Afro-Latin dancing a cadence a sensual movement hold your partner the fan tight in her hands, her white dress flowing, in the Danzón sway, bodies pressed tight. Great Afro-Latin musicians are still making people swing in dance halls, as some jazz innovations have moved toward the concert hall, leaving dance to the rhythm and blues folks. France ruled in New Orleans simultaneous with Haiti, slaves interchanged rhythms, Haiti was a fervent musical center, the French Contredanse jumped over to Cuba as eventually the Cuban habanera flowed into New Orleans. Remember that Jelly Roll Morton called it "The Spanish tinge," what Spanish tinge? Was it the Cuban tinge, what Cuban tinge? He meant the African tinge, which is what the Caribbean has preserved and transmits. New Orleans format (formation) of Jazz.

In the 1940s and 50s cha cha cha, mambo hit New York direct from Cuba, what eventually would be known as Salsa, a music derivative of African sacred rhythms of the Yorubas, Congalese, the Bantu, Mandingo peoples. The Cabildos and the Abakuá Society of African Cubans were essential in preserving rhythms, culture, religions, and the people held on to African cuisine, spiritual systems intact as in the Yoruba Lucumi Santería de Cuba or Candomblé of Brazil. Chano Pozo the conguero that worked with Dizzy Gillespie was an Abakuá Society member. The Voodoo of Haiti, in the eyes and hands of Marie Laveau dragging the giant snake Damballah through New Orleans the French Quarter which is Spanish architecture. Her Creole light skin of immense Africanía. The tinge is spirit stains, perfume, scent, psychological state, a walk, cake it if you want. It is possession of cool wind breeze, stance, gravity, holding the jumping horse, guiding it into paso fino tempo, sitting on your tongue that speeches poetry, sings as in language African words phrases, concepts intact in Cubano circles. What more cool than the Danzón? It predates the origins of jazz. Or like Ismael Rivera said in Puerto Rico "guembe mama quembe, habla quembe na mah" calling in his Africanized Spanish widespread through Loíza Aldea, a Puerto Rican community established by free Africans, perhaps among the first communities as such in the Western Hemisphere. Walk, camínalo, biscocho walk. Cake Walk, Andalusia guitar, Qué sabor, it is measure, power smoked into skins of drums, balance, a spirit which later funked into jazz. Proceed into Ragtime Jelly Roll and who more Rican/Cuban looking than Jelly Roll Morton, true criollo hitting the cinquillo note of the habanera, that lilt, motion snake horse swishing through the floor.

Jazz is not becoming Latin, that Africanía sway has always been an original essential ingredient since its origins. Jazz is like a Paella, everything can go into it. Thus jazz was a mixture and fusion of peoples of all ethnicities and colors. At the principio Sicilian Nick LaRocca Italian olive oil was founder of the Original Dixieland Jazz Band, Louis Moreau Gottschalk, Creole with Jewish blood from Anglo-London Papa, did he not stop into Puerto Rico, composed "Marches des jíbaros." Luis "Pepa" Tio, Mexicano and Creole, Danzón órale pues scoping the Mississippi which was clearer in this epoch. A migration to this Louisiana of Canary Islanders, bringing the décima poetic tradition with them, did they décima the blues. Islas Canarias, Spain in Africa. The "Mardi Gras Mambo" New Orleans where anything can happen, half the sea came into town, Katrina. Crime there like in all the other Caribbean localities, vicious with equality for all, rich or poor, blanco or moreno, if you looking for trouble you came to the right place, a vicious Manteca walking. The Caribbean a region of great oppressive policies by conquering Spaniards and subsequently other European powers, the total genocide against the Taino people who were exterminated in about two generations, the Caribbean today contains one of the poorest nations in the world, as in the nature of Haiti, one of the last colonial possessions in the world as is the situation of Puerto Rico with the United States, the only Communist/Socialist regime in the West as in Cuba. We are a region of extremes, yet a people's mestizaje and culture has arisen with a courage of survival, cultural triumph against all odds.

The great Jazz pianist of New York Rican descent Hilton Ruiz, who had been in New Orleans promoting an album which he participated in to raise funds for victims of Katrina, was assassinated on a visit to this northern edge of the Caribbean; thus indirectly Hilton was another casualty of Katrina. Mi hermano I will miss you for my whole ever. Lo and behold he went to New Orleans to share in musical goodwill, where jazz gave birth, with gospel, blues, and Latin Afro Caribbean elements, and he found his death. His Newyorican soul went marching out with the Saints, to dance rhythm with the Orishas.

Motion in the Silence

To the memory of Hilton Ruiz

A man puts Griffin on his white shoes
white guayabera hangs upon door hook
Bahía Matanzas not far, a salty powder
in the wind. Dance tonight above the plaza,
an ex cockfighting ring
converted into club
Now the roosters are men
the dance is the fight,
coquet the night conqueror,
the handkerchiefs wrapped around
the fans, the dresses so white
Milk next to them would appear
dark
Against skin warm moisture air.
going to town Pedro hoping
to see his desire flower
Teresa to be there, two days
back at the Mercado squeezing
Avocados she whispered to
him that she would, to find her
with her dress of white hilo,
holding her hand-painted
Sevilla fan,
He had seen her that afternoon
Moisture cheeks upon,
golden ruby skin sabrosa mulatta.
Grandfather from Galicia
mother hazelnut people probably
Senegal or the Congo deep,
a line of

Kongo mambo feet,
the maternal grandmother
high of Taino cheek
slant almond Asian eyes,
Tell me muses, oh tell me
what was Pedro looking at,
"Let the infinity stay without its stars,
But do not take from me her cinnamon"
Kisses,
thank you Bobby Capó
from Coamo on the Caribbean Sea
way across is Colombia,
"You are the one I care about
and only, only you"
"tú, tú, tú y tú no más
ojos negros, piel canela"
Mas Coamo composer where the girl
of society in the song "El Bardo"
fell in love with a poet,
absent the bard, the mountains cried.
all the rhythms were dressed as white birds,
clothes of the Caribbean to filter heat
the more luminosity flesh
covered as within Gardenia pétalos.

When his mother and father
took a steamship
cross the Caribbean
Mother eyes tear,
looking back on Saint-Dominigue
it was going to be a forever trip
father had a brother
wrote
to him about a job.

Now in New Orleans
some neighbors spoke French
some spoke Spanish
many already this new English
sound,
Nuevo dwelling not far
rounds the Mississippi flow,
they heard familiar drums in
Congo Square
walking begins day sunny
windy maybe rain
Afternoon,
he saw a girl reminded him of Teresa,
popped out hologram upon
the air sweet of colores,
A creole girl same Tere somewhere
else, else this same somewhere
is the where the equivalent again
becomes everywhere
moves duplicate rhythms
martillo between bongo
güiro y maraca
travel as to the drums
her eyes pierce
diamond arrows,
Orleans is the home of now
it matters not the local
But the drum,
the Caribbean a circle,
Bays and coasts
vanishing rivers,
the sway cadence like feet dancing
out of the water,
up, now down, to the side

brush
how it interferes with silence,
"Silencio the flowers are dreaming
I do not want them to hear me crying"
thus wrote Rafael Hernandez,
on the Caribbean coast of 116th St.
In Spanish Harlem,
the Savoy Ballroom not too far
Swing the Charleston, jump the Lindy Hop
Lindo, Swing, Jitterbug,
yo diddy-bops of old,
your bones aching with memories,
I recall Avenue D projects 10th Street
summer days walking along the rim
of the tenements
rose colored project bricks
adjacent brownish reddish gray
tenement brick montage, walking
My father's head above me as in the
sky like a cloud hanging
broadcasting his warnings, talking about
be careful, everything that shines
isn't gold, the consequences of your
actions, slowly you pay, Dios es el
que proporciona, it is God that
Proportions flesh on earth,
mix that with the sayings
of my Spiritual Grandfather
Don Arturo
"Sex" he explained with his shiny
white hair "is the most dangerous thing
in life, thus be careful,"
he was from Cuba and played guitar
music was his family.

One time slight snow upon street
walking this D Avenue
Going to club
80 Clinton, had my white shoes
inside the rubber boots
pressing white fluff snow.
Once there, salute the material
and search for the rhythmic spirit
of the Clave,
once found: mount
like a wave of the Caribbean going
toward the sand, not far Ponce
Where French last names circulate
tagged upon mulatos in barrio
Near the Sea
mix it up continue, sprinklings
Haitian French made it
Rico here as well,
to bomba explosions of Plena,
some song titles in French,
I am gliding like a Garza
wings white of guayabera shirt,
dancing with Teresa Morales.
Found her again,
Jersey City
black dress now, for winter clime.

Los marineros had seen Teresa
from the ships los marineros
immense white sails,
no name for her but Lola,
Aylelolelola,
The night improv begins
the Andalus said she waved,

later she dropped her handkerchief,
José continues, he almost died
wrapped in an embrace.
Golf of Mexico Portero New Orleans,
the Afro-Latin metropolis,
taking turns with French and Spanish,
was it further south Habana, Ana
Banana O Ana na nah, no mah
near Ponce arrebatah,
sandunguera, swaying dancing,
flowing with the saints,
when they came marching in.
A cleansing,
water rushing toward the drums,
I want to be in that number
when the Orishas come marching in.
with all that water alelujah, to bathe,
clean, Wash the head of Música

—*Cabio Sile Shango*

Egypt

I am far from Egypt sitting in a North African Moroccan living room, from some neighboring window pours chaabi music within another stream I hear the gimba bass guitar of gnawa music, mixing with the shriek of kids playing cora (soccer) out on the street. I've always wanted to go see the pyramids ever since I had knowledge of them; I have had to imagine them instead. In the Giza Plateau stands these pyramids, no one knows when they were constructed or even who did them and for what, why? Tombs for Pharaohs? No mummies found there. The pyramids must be instruments for the ether to play, funnels to create a sound, something invisible divisible flowing from way high beyond the moon beaming onto the earth, penetrating humans, deep organs and glands tickle nerves darkest interiors of creature bodies. Egypt was Africa's Mediterranean port, brown, yellow-white ginger tans, and a base of chocolate skin population. Nubians, Sudanese, the Middle East must've poured into Egypt the same way Latinos of Central America rain into North America today. The Yemens, Greeks, Turks, the hodgepodge of Middle East all in reach gravitated toward Egypt. Why not? The women in Egypt were beautiful. The beer was good. The social civic lifestyle more organized; employment, more security. Sounds familiar. History is like the Clave of Afro-Cuban music, infinite repetition; the clave originates in sub-Saharan African traditional music and dance. It is a time pattern, there are variations on the patterns, the most popular is the son montuno clave 3-2, it is the basis of today's Salsa music. All of Africa had influence from this root civilization of mankind: Egypt. The Dogon of Mali were founded by Egyptian priests, they carried with them the knowledge of science and cosmology. We could say religion was science, based on the practicality of natural forces. The position of stars and the certainty that everything is in rotation, is the heart pumping or is the blood rotating. Rivers flowing. The Astro Beings came out of the water, the Sumerians same boogaloo, the Incas speak of Viracocha jumping out of Lake Titicaca. The Egyptians were in tune with the glands and joints, what they call in India the Chakras. In certain Afrocentric circles there is concern about the color of the flesh of the ancient Egyptians, supposing them wearing skin as we know it, or were early on still ethereal, humid, vapor, or as the maestros that jumped out of the water half fish to bring them the light of knowledge. Maybe their skin was gray with fish scales. Did the Sumerians create writing first and it moved quickly through the Mediterranean? Humanity is so many questions without answers. Africans they were no matter the color they had. With chimes, flutes, cymbals, drums they danced, as people do the whole globe. Africa supposedly Latin/Portuguese word, the Bantus had another name, whoever the Bantu were, if not from Africa Whence? Kemo/Kemet exploded in the center and broadcast the Bantu, Bushmen scattering, those that pushed north became the Berbers, so many eons of years that passed all human types developed. But were the Iberians the Berbers and the Spanish peninsula or the Middle East part of Africa? Did it include elements of Celtic-Iberian? Thus the Gaelic Irish whom/what language spoke them. Some scholars have confirmed that when the Celts got to Ireland they found Berber North Africans there, or Spanish Iberians? Or blue people, Turquoise blond, black Tuareg people all invented by the Mother of the Tomatoes. The beauty of art, the jewelry, the clothing of the Egyptians cannot be denied, anyone with an ounce of aesthetic sense can see the advance culture that developed in North Africa. What was in that instance that we feel is not in any now contemporary moment, we are within the same ether, our glands and organs, body parts alike, are we not the same of that then here within this now. Pull ourselves back and bring them toward our nose, our hands painting the ojo of Horus with deep blue brush strokes. These were Africans the most essential truth. That is sufficient. White Berbers in Egypt were also Pharaohs. Color is irrelevant. What matters is the culture, the rhythm, the psychology, that is what the Caribbean continues to manifest, variety, wave after wave of our coasts. Such I feel was Egypt. It must've been a Santurce type of mestizaje. Yet the thought of Egypt disappears, breaks the frame of the mind. Where could we put the vanished time when the thought of space crumbles out: Stars.

Sopdet

The star is Sirius in the sky
night so bright
behind the sun
another sun,
a moon pebble weighs
more than the universe
a dance of couples
listen flute sound
Caracol
swaying, her lapis lazuli skirt earth
Hazelnut flesh in bright
light night.
Wrapped around
the scarf of my mother,
My father's word wind,
the philosophy of his proverbs,
planning direction of migration,
consulting the Bible,
It was the same everywhere
else space between rotating planets,
Babies born red with that
bluish stain above the splits
of the therma.
Traveling must've been
Dream body sunken in water
through eons of air,
Pasted somewhere
like you yucca starch
finalmente slam into stone,
clay scriptures caligrafic curves,
Horizon above sand continent
breath of mammals

approximates the limestone cave
electric swifts
Sound hints at matter,
formation blue rhythms
hear orange the sun falling,
listen to the twinkle bells
metal castanets
necklace of the sun
dancing around her ankle,
her face absorbed within
the black liquid of the night.

The pyramids are instruments
A penmanship upon limestone
trumpets, flutes of
medicine sound
curatives of colors,
seeing the turquoise stone
in the eyes of Isis.
Seeing the night
Maria in the sky
like light of day
upon black ether shines

Origin Egyptians/Ethiopios
below
blackness Gray fish skin texture
out of the sea into the day
And back at night sea sleep,
the first pharaohs divine
of Astro origin, feminine
feline
as Maser-Africa
was in the stars, the constellations

First whiffs of consciousness
were steps ballet with Osiris
Dancing
now mammals, mamaos,
breath hard for the
aspiring lungs.
Where was before
before it became,
was it hence,
backwards not even for impulse
desire for copulation
toward, prior desire.
If there was no
patterns to follow
moving the vessel through
infinite uncharted oceans,
more Isis sky the night
star twinkle.
Discover the instrument,
the Sphinx a head
older than the wind,
the triangles
just sound,
jazz create.
Was it the after of
a previous before,
to know we must
discover the imagination
of a lizard,
Eyes the total skin
radar for light,
(in a mountain house
tropical Puerto Rico
I lived with two green lizards,

became one with them,
a wall I had painted a bright
yellow tinge of gold
they never cruised through this
surface, por qué, elesh, why,
some realization inside cold blood,
occasions I tried to interview them,
to saber
wanted one day to touch
one as in a caress and it stood
still in anticipation/till whisking
nervously away off.
Yet it almost happened
it jumped toward the plantain
plant, guineos hanging like
birthing fingers a second
an instant before)
Was there a dinosaur jinn breathing
moisture near the passion fruit
trees,
lengua scribbles distortions
too velocity to capture.

A book of Egyptian myths in
my other hand
as I failed at my reptilian caress,
Osiris was with me
I fell in love with his wife
Isis
Who went after his offspring
raised the babies
of his puto urges.
Orgasmus of who whats.
Who-are.

The sky is the skirt of Maria
covering the naguas
Of Magdalena,
such is what is the star Sirius
hiding the other star
behind it
Though Eyes see upside down
everything looks fine backwards,
ophthalmologist thus spoke
I am looking forward to knowing
nothing,
Time exploded is the thought
of Egypt Maser
If it is coming
through the northern Mediterranean
the beam of Osiris
is flooding my living room
my fingers dance
with the Mama drums tumba
the gnawa gimba bass guitar
shukran to Aknathan
Singular of creation
Único Dios
sunken in poly-rhythms
Can dance
To echoes
A memory I can future
It is light lit like a
Star, nishma upon
the sacred mood.
Luz, Image
The cave is translation of the mountain
The pouch within, outside in.
Limestone walls scattered into green bush.

Babel: Allah.
MÚCARO.
GATOS
Everything upside down
Hanging
Solar Vegetable.
Resign:
Swallow light.

Tobacco-Guayaba y Café

Tobacco was used ceremoniously and leisurely in moments of relaxation by our Taino ancestors. Swinging hammock vision toward guayaba bushels adjacent spread of pineapples ass upwards toward the breeze. The aroma of the smoke carried prayers to Yukiyú, the creator; a wave of tobacco smoke enhances the path of communication. I was born in a tobacco town into a family immersed in the leaf. My mother's first job was accompanying Tina, her mother, to the big structure opposite the public plaza where the women took the large stem (palillo) off from the center of the leaf to create two halves, preparing the green leaf for the tobacconists. They called it despalillando tobacco. My mother's father Julio El Bohemio was a tabaquero; he rolled the cigars which in many of the Caribbean countries had become a labor akin to an artisan. It was more contemplative work, relaxed compared to other occupations in agriculture such as coffee picking or cutting cane, which are physically demanding. The tabaqueros as such were more serene in their task and persona. More cultured. Perhaps for this reason they had a reader come to lecture to them the newspapers, certain novels of the Spanish Época de Oro if not to recite poetry while they worked. My other grandmother on my father's side was Alejandrina, for short they would call her Lea, truly she had one of those Andalusian names which are abundant throughout Cuba, Puerto Rico, Santo Domingo. Soriada (in Arabic Soraya) Rebecca, Sonia, on and on. Lila, Layla, Lily, Lillian. Abuela Lea smoked and chewed tobacco. It was the Tobacco Criollo, the same one that Columbus's messengers saw the natives smoking in Cuba. I still have the memory of my abuela squatting smoking a cigar by a door in a place she had in Caguas. One of the last times we were together, she made me Goat Stew with white rice with a big slice of Avocado on top, the ones they say are like butter. I once tried some of her chewing tobacco while on an errand to pick some up at a local Aguas Buenas cafetín colmado, a drinking and dominoes hole known as Don Moncho's Cafetín, before getting back to her I cut off a piece and chewed some, nasty first thought, then dizzy wow am I going to vomit—faint next realization, bumping against walls as I got back to her sister Chencha's house where she was visiting. I drank water immediately she and Chencha chewed it all so smooth. My grandmother lived to be 86, another sister of hers called Chana lived to be 102, that clan lives long. They all smoked and chewed tobacco as the Taino spirit situation which they were in. They were frozen in that time frame.

My mother always made coffee at 3 p.m, it is an island ritual "el café de las tres"; she maintained this habit throughout our exile in New York, many years almost thirty. It was for me a great opportunity to sit with her and gossip. I would go down by the plaza to the panadería to get bread, some white cheese, or pastelillos de guayaba, perhaps besitos de coco. During this café ceremony we talked about everything, I used to like her to tell me about the town in the 30s and 40s, what has changed, what structures were there. It was during one of those coffee sessions that she told me how her mother used to take her to work despalillando tobacco down by the plaza. She told me about a Casino that was directly across the street from the tobacco place, how the popular music dance orquestas popular in those days would be brought in to form big dances, the jíbaras up in the mountains had to escape, make stories up to be able to go, mother gave me the details, she knew girls that had to cross rivers with their shoes in one hand the other hand lifting their pretty dresses, some girls made it to the edge of town and got upon huge horses till they got close enough to walk the rest of the way toward the rhythms. Café they say comes from Africa, that a shepherd from Yemen was in Ethiopia tending to some goats and saw them jumping and come alive after eating the greeny-red-orangy beans. He dealt with the issue till he extracted the juice, but it could be totally a different matter, could there have been Café in some of the past lost civilizations. Or in an Egypt lost to the tinieblas of time. I just know that my mother brought me up on fine coffee, even giving me a light mostly milk glass when I was but a boy. She used to use a colador, a filter which looked like a white sock which eventually darkened with use, the process was to boil the coffee grains in a pot of hot water and then pass it through the filter into a cafetera from which she could eventually pour it into the boiling milk, she always allowed the milk to rise which made the milk foamy. Coffee got us through many New York City snowstorms. Mami's favorite fruit was la guayaba, science tells us birth of the guayaba was across the water in the Amazona regions or within a region south of Mexico through Central America, quickly it made it to all Caribbean islands, way before the Latin patriarchal intrusion, I just know my instincts tell me that there is some fine bushels on a road toward Sumidero, a mountain barrio. She loved the guayaba paste, sweet beyond imagination, it is a sin no good for anyone no good for her diabetes, but we loved it, with crackers and white cheese forget about it. Oblivion.

Son las Tres del Café

Picture the aroma
memory before birth,
windows wooden boards
tranca
pushed out into the
sky of blue,
below the wood of the
floor slits
chickens squabble
bark dogs,
roosters jump, beaks
determination,
aroma
before sight to see/saw
in a somewhere imagined
before became, an air
gone shows stays
a picture eternal
past eating
vecinity
the next stop for the wind
is the river Guaraguao,
it carries with it the
tobacco dust lifted from
the worker's hands rolling
procedure,
add tint of café
and guayaba paste slices
cheese blanc
knife piercing
sweet jelly
the flavor tongue pores

suffocate,
motion vapors pronto
toward the cows
mesmerized by the terrain.
Road seeks the mountains
evaporate dancing into roble and caoba
trees. Night smoke stars.
Vanish, Lucifer appears
Amanece.

No more colador
now we Greca
Italian style espresso objective,
ground packed down
poignant accent speaks.
Café helps eye grab colors
nostrils open fill with morning
flower scents
Sol
ears wide acute to música
first drums, guitar and maraca shakes,
Caffeine haze the years
anxiety
rolls bottom of the ocean
Once again thank Africa
for café and homo erectus beings,
medicine beverage
encourages male pingola
stamina vigorón,
aid to reading, to the art
of looking at girls/women
who chance by street
Afternoon Café
as writing in the curves

of Egyptian hieroglyphs—
blossoming
in lizard green
notebook/Red Ink.

Chocolate

In Spanish or English Chocolate is the wind of Quetzalcoatl, the scent flavor of La Virgin Guadalupeña. Montezuma served a pure gold tass of Cacao liquid to Hernán Cortés, holding that gold sun in his hands full of choco, he realized and reaffirmed his conquering plans; after all, as he swallowed in amazement, where could this richness come from. The Aztec leader walking upon floors of jade, young wife's coming out of rooms ankles wrapped with turquoise bracelets hanging papagayo feathers, musicians' flutes songs like birds in chorus perfuming the air. Chocolate always brings me back to La Rondalla Mexican Restaurant in San Francisco's Mission District where once Californow time I tasted a taza of Mexican hot chocolate for the first time, it had cinnamon toning a ranchera tune within. The Olmecs in the dim of time prepared it with spices and chili peppers. Choco made it to Europe as did the tomato to liven up the Euro panorama (Roma-Italian what would it be without the tomato sauce) the Spanish the English is full of Nahuatl words, borrowed/Stolen. Bon apétit. History. What it does, who lives it, who writes it? What do we remember? Interpret. Chocolate modified, doctored, made less bitter addition of milk, come sugar. Milk Choco. Yet that something that is the center, what grabs at the taste glands is its native eternity, thus I am Taino resurrected each time I savor choco. I am Mayanized, Aztecolized. Mementos of California, recall the poetry of José Montoya and his Royal Chicano Air Force, they were Mexican astronauts poets who mixed the text with the folk loom of song, ranchera, balada, in the suburbs of American English or the center for those outside within.

Andre Segura Mexican scholar of the indigenous said it direct straight during a San Francisco State College lecture, the Maya/Aztecas came from another planet, they floated here, vaporized through space arriving like desire, ask the Egyptians, Sumerians, Babylonians, the Dogon peoples of Mali West Africa. They all sing the same song. The construct of human body non earth humane or godly natura engineering by fish figurines Sea out jump. Is there a star specific to chocolate? The god

Quetzalcoatl gave the secrets of chocolate to the people, other divinities became angry with him, reprimanded him, but he wise knew it was proper in time and space. Puebla people are made of chocolate, the mole a piquant chocolate sauce they make is a taste celestial divine full of spicy crunchy nuts, canela, chiles. It is a golden chocolate melt. Mornings in the future when I recall estancias in Fresno, California, circa the 70s band of poets and actors Festival of Teatro Campesino mornings of fruits and cups of chocolate or café con canela. Forever now those Chicano encounters are melted chocolate and canela in the cabinet of my memoirs, it was the birth of some of my poems, feeling those days and nights sunken in a dimension of an invisible Nahuatl ether oozing through reality. I cannot describe the sensation now in this English sprinkled with Spanish. Forgive my shortcomings; the tongue can taste what the lengua of sound cannot pronounce. Flavor there in indigenous time-atmosphere Feathered Serpent. The Fresno Valley immense earth is the food source of North America. The fruit, vegetables, pinto beans, corn as tortillas, food growing earth foot walking momentarily we are high above the fields soaring in flight, holding on to the eagle's neck, la Guadalupe standing hovering near all the doors protecting homes. Blue orange walls. Copal and vanilla, tamales fragrance begging nose open. Califlorica mornings of hazelnut skin breezes, chocolate paste cream between the teeth, taste glands upwards sizzling electric, has to be this divine Olmec heritage, afloat through the valley caressing white dresses flying hanging upon hazelnut color mestizas shining into the cosmos. Chocolate is another orgasm. Alive nascent bean enclosed-hidden within white creamy scum.

Choco-Arte

What if it wasn't what it is
color is not the setting
it comes in white
simulcast
Flavor supreme reality
taste does not suffer.
Montezuma drank
choco out of a cleaned
skull that used to be his enemy,
the wives of the skull
are thrown
back on jade posted beds
waiting silky for Montezuma.
Fairy tales of the
conquerors who stole the
gold of the Incas,
here we had the choco
and the contrast of vanilla,
the gold and the silver
feather panties separating
for night flight
spherical time the dance
Areyto rhythms,
Conch flute still salty
from the seawater,
why couldn't everything be squares
spinning must be shape in shape,
an intelligent origin choreography best
Shape that that of
leave it up to me.
Picture rectangular buttocks,
Geometric stalemate.

Flash flesh beauty,
natura guidance,
Atom baile rotate be it,
the word "round" is the symbol "O"
determination of itself, not it
as another unseen taste was
intent
but what's the matter
in the way,
an instant of twilight summer
emerges chocolate hint,
view mountain angle
firmament orange curve
sunken coastal fish colorete.
A shade of chocolate,
comes to imagine
night is actually a dark shady gray,
Whence
milky way enters mouth
no speech just awe opened
part salute part fright,
twinkle twinkle little star,
inside Cacao not too far,
equatorial belt
the waist of the planet
the sun a fertile woman
rays down to the Cacao fields,
kissing each night her husband
the moon.
Dance out of the Tropicana foliage
Tangle of vines
Somehow Articulate Chocolate:
Canta Lengua.

San Juan Bautista

Uncle José Antonio (Noño) has interned himself within the plaster of Paris Indian head that now Guane keeps in her old age, still talking to it, giving it fruits and fire. House in 40s was all wood Tina abuela cooking bacalaitos with green bananas was it a cent or two in that economy of bare obligation, no matter the situation we are all slaves of necessity. Mother got her labor pains fine tropical hot winter morning, not yet 7 a.m. by causality the comadrona-midwife Doña Lola was gracefully walking toward morning mass at the church adjacent the plaza, father called her over and explained the situation, she stayed and didn't leave till she gave me a slap and heard my crying. In dreams, see myself in the arms of my grandmother. Is it real reality or elusive imagination? Focus it, there it is! Abuela swaying me upon the hammock singing songs swapping at chance mosquitoes and flies with a rag. My mother took after her with the singing, it was a genetic disease. Rosa mother flower continued her song, sang to me even in the propeller plane which carried us to New York, fluffs of clouds looking solid like you could go out and walk upon them. Materializing in Manhattan we moved in time, the dream sleep changes air, what apparition have we entered, unexpected the snow, we were thrown like homeless Gypsies on the run from disfigured medieval painting of green mountains, vanished, we time machined into a new age; yet home is where the red beans boil so we made existence through the bricks, the language our Latin inheritance broadcasting through the walls cement bricks and steel, we made good strong café. San Juan Bautista was the original name of the island, it was renamed Puerto Rico way before my parents were born. Americans for a while boasted that we were the Showcase for Democracy, reality made all that propaganda obsolete. We went direct from Spain to the Americans, some Paris Treaty 1898 signed by no Puerto Ricans. History is outside of us, thus we pretend, are we trying to get in. Once I heard the independentista Carlos Gallisá speaking to Lehman College students, one of the students asked him if Puerto Rico could survive without the United States and he shot back that the real question is will we survive with the United

States. In this epoch of the imminent collapse of the island the question has been answered. Manifested. Now we are in such deep mush mud that we must recuperate our Caribbean being, proclaim our varied ethnic cultural possibilities, and wear all our colors. We are layers of civilizations thrown like blankets one on top of the other, or we polish that up or vanish. Taino/Spanish/African stew that we are we can sing dance, cuisine eat it, munch. Island natural beauty now as the island depopulates, last one out shuts the lights off. Coquís, toads, and lizards will be the last occupants, cold blood reptiles the figures registered in the final census. Sangre Fría. Many of my dear friends are clamoring for independence of the island, to be a republic, that we are just another Caribbean Latin American country. How historical so truth. Yet the actual reality of the world is that there is no such thing as an "independent" country, that all so-called free republics are intertwined, interrelated one to the other, such is the case of the United States, France and England, China, Japan, India, Russia, etc., they all thrive and exist through trade, partnerships, economic industrial and cultural exchanges. The best economies are those that mix systems, within somewhat socialist ideas. Recent developments in the situation of Tibet and its relationship with China are encouraging, the Dalai Lama has sat down to negotiations with the Chinese government, the Tibetan government in exile has agreed to certain Chinese demands, explicitly that Tibet is an integral part of Chinese history. Many other issues still have to be worked out. Why can't the Independence people of Puerto Rico approach the United States government in an analogous manner as the Tibetans have done? Thus we will behold if the U.S. will even allow the protocol of dialogue. The Independence movement of the island does not constitute a separate government, there is an Independence Party led for decades by Rubén Berríos, and some organizations which struggle for an independent state.

Can they grow to demand that Puerto Rico become part of the interdependency of the world negotiate with the Americans in the various proportions, economics, language, and culture, geopolitics, environment to achieve this? Look at the United States and see what it is really. And realize what Puerto Rico actually is, the proportions, the topicality. The nature of nature. Thus I would desire the same destiny for my island nation, to become politically an interdependent country as is the reality of the actual world. Those clamoring for "independencia" are taking a retroactive position that would place us in an isolated frame within an island which has no natural resources. A minor workforce. Que viva la Inter-dependencia the actual future of now. This is the way the world is. We want to be world. Y Cosmos.

Puerto Rico

Born on a turf
a medieval remnant
Owned by the United States,
it was almost water
So minute the earthen formation,
barely rock,
a swift of natura intention
geologic lift forgot the mud load
as the rising slow, eruption
popped
peep there it is piedra Caribe,
world mapmakers save
on the ink,
what minuscule elaboration
bays, lakes,
hidden caves
landscape, chains of mountains
opening blue neck of sky
mounted glued
alongside other Hispano-Caribbean isles
Santo Domingo/embracing Haiti
Cuba bird snake long,
Spanish-African movement.
the Federation which
Betances the doctor clambered for
the Antillas Españolas,
intellectual political Independence.
Some letter bestowing Puerto Rico
sovereignty
from the Spanish Crown
the United States no desire
to open that envelope.

Betances visionary mestizo
Paris his doctor's foot.

The epoch of gold
when on the island with my son
we made home,
in the neighborhood of
the tobacconists
Aguas Buenas
on a street called Antorcha
a socialist flame
of the independentistas,
workers barrio of chinchales.
My family there Generations.
The mornings waking my son
for school,
watching him become a man,
awakening sense to life,
his first girl kisses
that pretty brown girl
primer girlfriend
I spotted them once
wrapped round each other,
like two bacalaito fritters
tangled,
later my mother cooked
Red beans and plantain tostones
along with yellow rice sparked with corn,
The island was this sofrito flavor for me,
bolero music of my mother
she grew sadness with the lyrics
wondering of all the lost loves,
memories illusions making
efforts to materialize,

see them almost
like bridges hanging out
from her eyes.
Days were
found her in tears
lonely in her room
Fragrance of Florida water
circulating blue colcha,
picture of her mother
and father above bed,
nothing was ever coming,
the only future was the end.

The Caribbean is everywhere
lost within us,
trapped in kitsch glorious
rooms of plasticity jails,
so much grime 'tween
the beauty contra-la-danza,
René Marqués our writer
Belched out
"Condenao mar, tanta agua
Y no limpia nah"

Through the bullets
flying now in panoramic tropical
scenarios,
Mother kept singing,
as esperanza, gently vibrato
hope like a white
Garza landing upon a cadaver.

Humming
songs forever

soothing.
convinced
she would meet
everyone she knew
in heaven again.
Singing boleros
café con leche,
Pastelillos de Guayaba.

To the bad times
give a happy face,
place a red amapola
in your black dark hair.
Revive the mummies,
the dead,
burst the bodies
out of the coffins
let's all walk to the plaza
this final time
paint with silver starlight
the ancient songs
in night sky,
Rain Again
What never commenced
Comes to a finale.

Borges y Nabokov

I have read Borges and Nabokov since the early 70s in places-cities that have erased themselves, forgotten me, and altered. It takes many readings and changes of geographies and as growing beings becoming to appreciation, comprehension. Reading is also mood connections with the writer, the sentence and the paragraph collide with the environment during my sunny bright days of Puerto Rico tropicality, with the dim winters of New York survival of snowstorms a book, words, ooze out of the urbanity of the contemporary toward voyages of timelessness. With books you have to live with them for duration of spaces, changes of geographies, and changes in women, moods, and attitude shifts all contribute to expansive horizons of awareness. First I spotted the *Fictions* in the library of Ms. Karen Kennerly who was the secretary of Herbert Kohl at the original Teachers and Writers Collaborative working with alternative education in New York City; she was fascinated with the Argentine writer and communicated the enthusiasm to my young waking mind. It was an English translation, at the time my Spanish was mostly oral, over the years the literate part of my Spanish awoke and I re-encountered Borges's *Ficciones;* reading him in Spanish was like discovering a new Borges sense, even though Borges was close to the English language, his father and one of his grandmothers spoke to him in English as a growing child. Borges is the kind of writer that you have to read and reread over the years as your own comprehension evolves. Some Borges stories have a flavor of essays; it would be wise to be informed of some Greek and German Philosophers, Eastern-Arabian texts, and listen to some Tangos to get a better grasp of this Latino formation at work. There is a saying in Spanish to the effect that "the Mexicans descend from the Aztecs, the Peruvians from the Incas but the Argentinians descend from the boats" because of the large influx of European migrants into the southern cone of America Latina. Borges is old stock criollo and on occasion has mentioned that because he doesn't have Italian blood he feels like a foreigner in his own country. Reading him has always been such an elevation of perception while at the same time he walks you through a macho bar of black mustache compadritos drinking throwing measure left and right, penetrating the black dresses of the women with eyes like razors slashes/ slicing the material. The most important element of all art is the concentration, musicians, painters, writers; poets have a concentration like slow honey dripping in a planet with no law of gravity. I can feel that focus in these two pregnant writers, Borges taking his time writing about time, Nabokov exploring desire, writing a book about writing. Though we could say that *Lolita* is about sex—old man young girl, pretty universal— in the mechanics of the prose it has always been for me a book about artistic creation. Lolita is the muse flesh alive. Nabokov (Humbert his character) bathes her, takes her slow in all the angles, wonders at his own fascination, keeps a mirror on the adventure, inside of him the red fire, outside cool-coldness forecasting the distant society and what might those criminals think. They have such laws that restrain pleasure, movement, freedom, lucidity, adventure, Eros. Nabokov was also the eternal exile; Russia was a place he never returned to, St. Petersburg permanent melt like a fresco in the foreground of his thoughts, always present in all his writings, he had to recreate it, live off his memories. One of his prose works is called *Speak, Memory.* I have read the books of Borges y Nabokov in a Morocco of Mediterranean cool to cold winter times; the cold here reminds me of the cold of San Francisco, a humid coldness not cold sufficient for snow, but a bothersome insistence, it acts as an implosion seemingly getting into your bones and finally trying to break back out. Heat the chilly out, with mint tea or café during the natural light of day read Borges or dive into the bright careful prose of Nabokov read into the silence of the night as I have always done to get my eyes tired for sleep. Borges is always philosophy and Nabokov is moral politic, the human customs, underneath the colors painted hidden. Desire. History moves through the intrigues of both, a place a time, characters are nations, epochs, settings. Reality a crime to dissect as in Borges detective stories. Borges wrote some poems with English titles, but he remained faithful to the tongue of Cervantes, he spoke English well and some German. Nabokov abandoned his Russian even before coming to America he was already in English expression. These two writers have kept me company for decades, when I read them at first, not understanding, but as changes came to my own life awareness kept rising, their books open up with new meanings and vigor, geographies and moods change your perception of words-wor(l)ds, the same word a different world. It never settles down anywhere.

Lectura

The black ink
dances with the white
sky of the page
scribbling the footsteps
of the dancer
pensive swirls on the flow,
the tapping of a bastón
Between the rhythms of
the walk.
The Argentinian proceeds
in the haze of dark-milonga
Some slivers of light
enough to discern a house
or a tiger in front
pending.
A writer, a collector of literature
gatherer of legends
Flowing with and against the classics,
a tourist always
in the realm of the Tango
bars of the port, Portuario
Buenos Aires,
night alegre of swift feminine.
In *The Book of Sand* Borges
Pointed to the Habanera Cubana
As the origin of Tango.
In the salon dance
I only read the silk
and the red lipstick
the outline of speech.
Enjoy the tilt of the steps
knives of the mustache,

the black dress swirls
pressing against the
black panties,
the netted socks
rise like
Geometric squares painting,
arithmetic of desire-baile
upward nalga tinges of
skin porcelain tan ginger,
black stockings
reverberation dizzy of the squares,
Latinos all the ports
black café rises from the Greca,
La China, Averroes Andalucía
The two circles of the word
Moon in English,
German of Goethe the moon
is a man.

Viejo I disagree with you
on Lorca
dismissed him as mere folklorist
A painter you said,
in the story "La Secta del Fénix"
Without mentioning his name
You scribed "Los gitanos
son pintorescos e inspiran
a los malos poetas"
but I rise with "Poet in New York"
mornings of mint tea bread dipped
in Olive oil my Berber stance
in the chills of North African
Mornings
the section "Calles y Sueños"

el Granadino hints of Arab blood
opens free in Vein-Verses,
previous tradition peninsula rhymes
sliding down the walls of
The Alhambra.

Other momentos I understand
Borges,
if focus upon *Romancero gitano*
folklore enclosed,
the customary coplas
sing themselves, into color
Bright
Lorca's paintings hang
in the museum of my memory.
Spain stain like
ancestral Nasari blood,
Granada swimmers
Latin/Arabic
in the sea of dawn New Dialect:
Castilian: Spanish.

The same words of Borges
tangano of accordion/guitars
Another country/time
old encyclopedic. A Swiss
watch mechanic at labor.

Each time I scope a butterfly
I think of Nabokov,
from a Caribbean balcony
upon glance saw groups
Of yellow flowers flying,
coming from the river

headed toward the mountains.
Season is that I caution to
avoid stepping on Caterpillars
Orugas
so as not to destroy paintings
in process
their souls fidgeting
with shape design,
the symmetry of desire,
one caterpillar looked like it had
the haircut of the British rock
group The Beatles.
Vladimir discovered new species
of butterflies
such was the concentration
The leisure.
the estate in Saint Petersburg a valley
comfortable prairie vodka extension of
liquid papas.

Ithaca New York dreamscapes,
warmer winters for him.
Seasoned writer would never
action upon a young girl,
but thought profoundly upon it
La ninfa to commit the sin
of his "loins," in writing, ah Lola
atrévete, ven otra vez
ponla al revés,
Lolita was his writing muse
La Beatrice, his Dulcinea
for me *Lolita* has always
been a book about writing,
encounters illegal suspense

plotting intense scenes of pleasure.
"Ada" another Latina name
momentos of sharp scenery
exhaustive narrative,
narrow down to his "13 Stories"
crossing the Atlantic my airplane
warmth, the cold ocean below,
wind, clouds form y dissolve,
page turn time watch stare
soar like a bird frog
jumping rock to rock,
New York/Casablanca
New York/Madrid
again Madrid/New York.

Un moment Vladimir
what you mean you don't
like jazz,
Sit down careful to listen
same way read Dickens's
Bleak House   what?
he wrote of his distaste
for Jazz-music in *Speak, Memory.*
So many times
read him with soft
Thelonious Monk ballads
Sunken floating in the back
improvs of jazz crawling
down like roaches wall
words in piano concert with his prose
keys
insects marching line vertical, now
a left turn to where, antennas sonar
aware of distances and texture

insinuations, sudden drops of
the plaster of Paris paint,
occasions of caves-wall bumps
where the temperature alters.
Hot episodes of hands
usage finger popping manual
vagina virgin
pages like new hair
of Lolita or Dolores
of my pains,
auburn prose
of lost Russia,
grandiose St. Petersburg.

Federico del Sagrado Corazón de Jesús García Lorca

Known in the world of literature as Federico García Lorca, referred to popularly as Lorca, the last name of his mother. In the Latino tradition we use the last names of both parents, the middle name is always the father's and the most important of the names. For some reason his maternal last name prevailed. The quiet and shy Andalusian poet born in the sector Fuente Vaqueros, a large extent of rural land of Granada, a farm area owned by his father. His mother taught school locally and was a piano player, a skill that she passed on to her son. Lorca's youth was full of the music of Debussy, Chopin, and Beethoven. As a lad he made relations with flamenco, helped to organize concerts and competitions. He was a close friend of the composer Manuel de Falla; we could say that Lorca is a good example of a musician turned poet; he was also a gifted graphic artist. He flirted with Theater some years till he finally settled into writing poetry and essays; his theater pieces were eventually published and have been performed throughout the entire world. Lorca was sent on a journey to America by his wealthy family, he boarded the *SS Olympic* a ship à la Titanic along with his friend and teacher Federico de los Rios, their destiny was New York City. In New York he enrolled at Columbia University and ran smack into the cold climate of the people, the hurried indifference, the anonymous hordes, rows of ants marching mindless, yet he was excited by the bubbling metropolis. Theater his main interest, New York City great Broadway of the Teatro like a feast for his mind, as afternoons were of solitudes writing to melt the skyscrapers. Took notes observed fascinated the joy of his youth, the Caribbean was not far and the tropics were calling him as well, took another ship to Cuba joined the rumba there; in Santiago he heard the music and observed the dancers. In New York he had met Langston Hughes and in Cuba he encountered Nicolás Guillén. Lorca was alive with new forms sprouting as he opened up into free verse. The style of the *Gypsy Ballads* what turned Borges off, he saw the gypsy as a theme, something raw that he reached for, his friend the filmmaker Luis Buñuel criticized the work didn't round well into Lorca's folklorist attitude, Salvador Dalí more supportive saw it as just a phase his friend was going through; there are within the *Romancero gitano* poems of fine imagery, the color, love desire death, jealousy themes so ever present in Spanish culture poignant in Andalusia, essence in Lorca. I had the honor to be invited along with Judith Ortiz Cofer* and some other writers by the Fundación Federico García Lorca, which was housed in the facilities of La Residencia de Estudiantes, the famous school of the 20s which was host to many of the important literary figures of Spain as students and professors; Juan Ramón Jiménez was a teacher there, Pedro Salinas, Lorca, Salvador Dalí, Luis Buñuel. They were all young, full of energy and excitement, they exchanged ideas, Dalí and Buñuel plotted together the film *Un Chien Andalou*. The ideas of the twentieth century were explored as something modern was happening. We met family members of Lorca like Manolo Montesinos and Laura García, both had spent time in the United States and spoke English with an Americanese swing. From Madrid we ended up flying with the family to Granada and in Fuente Vaqueros saw the old family house still in the rural setting, entering we beheld some of Lorca's paintings hanging and an old piano settled in the living room. Back in Madrid at the Residencia where we stayed the dorms we were in were the same rooms once habituated by Dalí, Lorca, Salinas, Juan Ramón; we never found out which rooms any of the particular poets might have inhabited, but it was a special excitement to be within so much histori-cal creative air. Walking Granada with the Lorca's beholding Middle Age structures popping along with the modernity. Splendid sights to behold from windows, as we drank rum and danced salsa, out the window was the Grand Mosque of Granada, feeling all the time the spirit of Federico amongst us. Granada con-con-gana.

Judith Ortiz Cofer—Puerto Rican American author of novels and essays just passed away. I hereby recall that she went to Lorca's house with me. Sweet of temperament beautiful Judith your words always in my eyes, spirit more ever within heart. Descansa.

Cante Jondo

To Laura García and Manolo Montesinos

The tongue makes
a trembling sound
moving as in a wet kiss.
Moisture is the Granada
afternoon people of ginger
flesh, dresses fly like red
Rioja wine flags in
the precious air, preciosa
that I want you such
Green
Green desire yearns
"Verde que te"
eye suck color shapes
Andalusia black hair
Arabic culos night thighs
of moon circles.
There visiting with
Laura y Montesinos
familia de Lorca
in Charge of La Fundación
Lorca at the Residencia
de Estudiantes
where infinite drinks of
cultura were swallow flow,
the dorms one room Salvador Dalí,
another Pedro Salinas,
somewhere the dormitorio of
Maestro Juan Ramón Jiménez,
convulsive afternoons in the
free experimental school

a Latin Oxford,
John Cage sound music
slicing through the books
of Breton's surrealism,
whatever Lorca, Salinas
were reading, Azorín, *La Celestina*,
Mio Cid, el Hugo, the French.
Morning jump with excitement
questions of the night before
poetry is memory of
inquiry desires just so many
questions, begging
the possible colors.
that respond.

Einstein spoke there
relevant to relativity,
of what gravity the pull of
Grammar, the buttons and pins
commas, dots, commas mark
of question entry sentence
upside down erect finality
Castilla.
Of lengua the glamour, decor
standard yet personal
once you know the scale
you can break it.
Blow as John Coltrane,
Albert Ayler leave it alone.

Juan Ramón el Andalus universal
Modernism at its edge.
come the fascist hordes of Franco
Juan Ramón ended in Puerto Rico

on the island he died
rested a while when Franco passed
his family took his remains
back to Spain, as he had wished.
Pedro Salinas arrived on the
island as well to contemplate
the sea, the insistent waves,
the black hair Marias
morenas
in the tropics they come in
cinnamon skin, trigueñas.
The seashells of his metaphors
mixing philosophy with the Carib,
Salinas too died in Puerto Rico
and remains resting by the
eternity of the ocean waves
Inspiring,
his bone feet pointing
Everness
toward the azulie waves.

In 1932 Agustín Lara
the Mexican composer
wrote the song "Granada"
the song sailed into my ears
from a distant window
while I sat in the Residencia
reading loco Lorca local,
invoke the shine of orange flesh
Illumed out of black shawl.
The walls of la Residencia
melted memoirs,
such possibilities,
for those who ate air,

composition of the mountain
persona
springs into river currency,
Now
Lyrics of Johnny Albino
Come from the depths. Caverns
Caribe gone, alive but . . .
"Dios quiera que tu vayas,"
If you remember of me,
Sonos of the language
Scape in Eye
Living again/
Uno nunca se puede ver
The past is futuring,
"Fatalidad ah vives"
Motion stand
If there dance,
It now when.
The function is seen
Been Andalucía Granada*
Kalendro.

*Garnāṭah *the Arabic name,*
From the Persian for pomegranate.

Don Quijote

The cold upon such mornings caress the fingers of this North African winter. The debaba-fog of the Mediterranean floats above the medinas hazing, twirling, dimming the geometric tiles rushing towards the water fountains, cool cats darting in the crepuscular dawn light. The cold enters through your nostrils and all the pores of exposed flesh, it rushes quickly to the center of your bones from which it eventually escapes back out. It is an implosion. That is where the mambo is. Mierda I am translated here shit from the tropics trembling. In Africa mofos. Realize that my whole life is translation, first it was from bucolic town to the inspires of New York buildings, reaching, growing with time a jump from the East to the West Coast. Everything translates transforms. Current in Morocco above us is the Mediterranean, flamencos between Europe and Africa. My family house here is translation, with my woman and my son we move in and out of the Spanish, the Arabic, the French always deciphering content, English bounces around as well. It is how we function as family reviewing words so that we are all on the same page and in comprehension. The three of us bump into words, review them translate them back into the Spanish which is our base language. Up before the 6:30 a.m. call to prayer on a cold November morning I open the huge Bible like book of Don Quixote in English translation. The translator of this English version is Edith Grossman. She has translated mostly contemporary Latin American writers, García Márquez, Mario Vargas Llosa a couple that I know of. To tackle this monster from the Middle Ages she must've taken more than one deep serenade of siestas; I kept going back from the Spanish version to the English and I could see that she captured the spirit of Cervantes's voice, made it echo in our contemporary "Americanese" English as she herself comments in a beautiful little book *Why Translation Matters:* "Good translations are good because they are faithful to their contextual significance. They are not necessarily faithful to words or syntax, which are peculiar to specific languages." Translating Spanish to English I have discovered that many times in English you have to put the phrase backwards, turn it inside out for it to make reading sense. Edith has captured the spirit of the language and manages to paint it over into English. Delightful. This reading in English of el Quixote would be my second reading; there is a saying in Spanish that the novel *Quixote* has to be read three times in one's lifetime, once as a youngster, another during middle age, and finally another time as you age and are cured like a good bottle of Rioja wine. My first reading of the book was back in the hot moisture of Puerto Rico, swinging upon hammock the back balcony of my mother's house in el Barrio El Guanábano, a popular neighborhood, listening to the boleros and the Salsa flowing from a local cafetín (small bar) and the sound shuffle of the dominoes upon an old worn wooden table, I had hung a Taino hammock there for the very purpose of reading, and I do declare a hammock as the best place to read a book, it is a uniqueness like it invented the distinctive singularity of the float of lectura, the ease of shifting body positions, outdoors with the natural light of the tropical day has no comparison, my favorite reading time was and is always in that part of the day when the sun is sliding down, I would read till the darkness made it impossible to proceed. Finally the black ink of the letters melts into the dark tinge of the approaching night. Strung out in the Caribbean wondering about the small enclaves of Castile de la Mancha. Voices from the local street mix into the Middle Age drama "mira Mariano está abierto el Checo" horizon yonder the breasts of the mountains sprout alongside villages Albacete, la Mancha fortresses and merges castles out of the landscape, sudden a house appears en la meseta forms levels from which pours a barefoot girl named Minerva walks to my nose a musk of deer horns hay wire, in the barrio there is Sonia brown and auburn hair, OJOS. The prose encloses me in a cocoon; distant geographies appear-disappear, stretch of isolated mountain villages, is it there or is it here, cuál? Mountain people everywhere signature the same, Don Quixote de la Mancha de Plátano. One night it was dark late yet I wanted to continue reading, I was somewhere in the outskirts of Toledo, a huge lake during sun fall gave it the semblance of dark blue ink, turned the balcony lightbulb on, two pages pass when I hear a sound, swish swift noise it was a Praying Mantis out of the night the size of a helicopter with its green cape slams into the wall next to me, next a flying roach huge, eventually insectology-bichos of weirdest categories, slaves of light arrive in waves, objects with no names that I can think of, I had to get back in before I got bitten, eaten, or something. The publisher of Cervantes's book sent most of the copies to the New World to the Americas, to the new Spanish lands, a shipment of them was swallowed by the ocean off of Havana, it was the early 1600s, the fish read the soaked text, a batch made it to Lima, Peru, from there El Quixote arrived into Cuzco, center of the Incas. Cervantes was planning to come to the Spanish Americas last years of his life but he never realized it. His book made it, phenomenon. There is in the novel Muslim-Morisco characters and situations, Zoraida, Hebraic insinuations, Cervantes even invented a fictitious Arabic author to whom he attributed the second half of the novel published ten years after the first part appeared. The novel was set within the drama of the Moors and Jews being expelled from Spain. I had heard of El Quixote all my life, it sat in the culture, in the language, and people talking would mention it. Unamuno called it a second Bible. My first reading of this novel, I burnt into the gravity of the language, the situations and the settings of the novel, the characters set in the Middle Ages yet sounding so immediate to me as I was turning the pages, encountering my own barrio experience. How many times swinging in the sway of the suspended hammock did I not sail into sleep and awake in a dream of El Quixote. Sueño.

The Ingenious Gentleman Don Quixote de la Mancha

Listening to a voice,
is it inside of me or outside?
Is it the candle my mother
lit to the Milagrosa,
talking to me?
sound is coming from the
Crucifix
above and behind
the dancing flame,
is it the alphabet that
makes the words, each letter
each syllable
The language is what talks.
Is the whole Romanesque/Latino
Arábico off its hinges.
An old lady is balcony talking
has not stopped yapping
two days now, neighbors
resorting to witchcraft
Make the old bitch stop,
what they call in Spanish
Refunfuñar, bickering equals it
In English can't approximate,
listless speech, spitting irritation
pestering
I sin sity que jo sin sity.
Alonso Quixano reminds
me of my uncles,
highfalutin boisterous
fiery, excuse for any conflict.
Quijote in one scene said
to a particular,

"I'll jump off this mule,
and split you in half"
The loud voice threat
enough more sharp,
Valiente as art,
pendeja if has to be,
be it, you could have just
formed a circle, let me
and the guy understand each
other, uncle Juan.
If they not fighting moving
buildings
or a loose lion on Avenue Be
it's not for nothing not,
a lion has escaped in the zoo
and logical it is to zoom, Raul.

The mirror lies to me
tis not the gallant cojones
testicular macho,
other uncle Carlos
said face his in mirror
offended him and he slapped it
blood drops hand.
Who was that abuser shameless?
Huge green iguana came
to the balcony I had to lift
up from an inferno of books,
the niece the priest
burning picaresque novels
claiming readership
made Quixote sick.
Reading is bad for you,
Give way to music

Silent images in motion,
go for sword or masterbate.
Crushing, pictures pile up traffic
Jam thought airport.
In North African Algerian jail
voices to Cervantes came,
jail brings you closer to language-words,
Love letters to whomever,
Malcolm X got to reading the
Dictionary,
loneliness is the fire of language
there's only you and it
under an ocean of time
repetitive like an eternal clave,
when inside the scenes rolling
Deck of cards.
El lenguaje becomes transparent
passage through, time erases.
The task of reading becomes light
transparent, when
I am home the coquí toad
dotting sonic space like stars
over the mountains,
Don Quixote hangs there
Don Q de la Mancha
De Plátano.

Reading Japanese in Morocco

"No oil to read by
I am off to bed
But ah . . .
My moonlit pillow"
    —*Bashō*

I have always admired Haikus, I compare them to having little money
and you have to enter into a grocery store and get the ingredients to com-
pose a meal, thus select with the little there is wisely. Robert Hass's *The
Essential Haiku: Versions of Bashō, Buson, and Issa* has been with me as con-
stant companion since it came out around the mid 1990s, it was with me
in Puerto Rico for years of morning café, along with the nightly singing
of the coquís. Some of the nights of Bashō, Issa nearby owl mooing sit-
ting on a lonely Guavara tree or was it a Guayacán árbol of Taino dark
wood. My left elbow juncture bone point has stained itself dark from
pressing upon it during my nocturnal bed reading, a bad habit I just have
to live with; here in Morocco Senegal people in the old Medina sell some
good Shea butter which I pick up to rub into the stain agony of my lec-
tura. Once in New York I picked up three Japanese novels, *Snow Country* by
Yasunari Kawabata and *A Personal Matter* by Kenzaburō Ōe and *Nip the
Buds, Shoot the Kids.* Kawabata was born in Osaka in 1899 and died in 1972
supposedly committing suicide a la Yukio Mishima who was his partner
in right-wing politics, something about a gas stove. His wife denies the
whole suicide bit. Blames his death upon some gas stove malfunction.
Whatever happened he is stiff dead, his body that is. Both of these writ-
ers have received the Nobel Prize for Literature, Kawabata in 1968, mak-
ing him the first Japanese to obtain this award. Kenzaburō Ōe was born
in Uchiko, an agricultural region. As a child his mother gave him the gift
of the American classic *The Adventures of Huckleberry Finn*, assuring him
a lifelong influence from Mark Twain. Kawabata along with the writer
Yukio Mishima signed a petition against the Maoist Cultural Revolution
in China whereas the left wing leaning Kenzaburō gave it full support,

even visiting China. Kenzaburō took influence from the French philosopher Sartre, existentialism something I could never understand, I had a copy of that big book *Being and Nothingness* in the 60s, but I was not analytical enough to penetrate the polemic, some people do and well many blessings to them. A friend of mine had told me to read *Snow Country*, aware as he was of my love for the Haiku form, indeed the Novel's prose is like a necklace of haikus, a "renga," as a Japanese critic called it. The scenes pace themselves slowly, a cadence of paso fino which was translated by Edward G. Seidensticker, he translated not words but space-air-timing, the Japanese scholar and translator of many great Japanese works including *The Tale of Genji* in 1976. Seidensticker speaking about the translation of *Snow Country*: "You translate not just the words but the rhythm as well"; in other words you translate silence. I would imagine you translate the temperature as well, turning the pages I felt many whiffs of cold mountain snow air, even while reading segments in tropical Puerto Rico. The lonely freaky mountainous isolation zone, a feeling that you are sunken within an immense cold white stretch of earth scattered hotels, inns, rich lonely men, geisha girls, putas not exactly though the melody can be played. The character in the novel Shimamura a cultured man who loved the ballet, refined, making observations, young girls rattling through snow in kimonos. Komako his geisha vaporizing sake, dizzy of desire, snow drunk feel the chills evermore even. Like ice cubes the prose tumbles down into you until you apprehend the tragic avalanche you are frozen in, a prose precise, ice staring at the mountain snow tips. It shines cold sun. Slow honey dripping upon frozen chrysanthemums.

Chuchuki

It's not guacamole,
Sure by now
You've found out
This wasabi shit
Not hot sauce
Rather some kind of vapor
It creates an implosion
Inward nostril
Tsunami next
As Brains spills
Down your nostrils,
Turns you insides out
The first rush
Survive that
Proceed with the meal.
I had some chuchuki
San Francisco
Red kimono
She spoke Spanish.
Books are paper
Wild timber tamed
Trees in your hands,
Wonder if they have lice
Mealybugs, termites.
In the Caribbean books aging
Heat moisture
Yellow spots grow
Makes a stank of mildew.
I am witness to print
That moves
Periods who stride
Meaning till the comma sleeps,

As such changing
The sentence-meanings,
The pace, apostrophe rests into semicolon
Like a question mark elaborated,
Minute creatures persist,
A particle of dot dust,
An organism partial to books.
Bamboo thin of tropic forest
Air.
Cool winter Maghreb
Paper holds better
Mediterranean ether
Reading the Japanese novel
Kawabata *Snow Country*
An isolated distant cold looms.
Are there people in town
Or frighten bones struggling
Toward hot spa water,
Geisha serves tea
In magenta kimono,
Ah what breast-less
Breathless beauty,
Buttock curve like
Shushi tuna rolls,
Something is aesthetic happening
Through the whiteness
The writer makes you see:
"The road is frozen. The village
Lay quiet under the cold sky...
The moon shone like a blade
Frozen in blue ice."
How chuchi can you get,
The prose throughout
Links of Haiku pictures,

Slow peeling strips
Of apricot, cheek tongue
Labios blood red
Tumbling lengua in mouth,
Black hair silk shines.

Kenzaburō transmitted
A delight through my
North African icy fingers
Hanging on to: "Nip the buds,
Shoot the kids":
"Then the girl's small face
Appeared-red with fever
And with the down from
Her cheeks to her ears shining
Golden"
The no sense is non-logical
Sense it makes sense Since
In the cup of tea: it is taste.
Image rolls flickering
Measured shape colors,
Bud growing flowers,
Music like the
Zen spells of koto long zither
Meditations,
Bamboo by the river
Wind flutes color
Sounds.
I've long trips gone with
Bashō who is a road
Through cherry blossom springs,
The Spanish refrain
"Por si las moscas"
Mosquitoes/butterflies

Sapo/frogs
The chance
Knowledge comes suave
On a wave of obvious
Invisibility.
Geisha secret better
Than the mafia.
A rose like the
Waves of a fan
Within red,
Medina window view Mountains.
Language fades
Words diminish
As an alphabet
Sticks upon
Two little Sapo
Bashō
Frog/Legs.

Splash.

Chess

First time I saw a game of chess when I was young street kid Lower East Side hanging out at the Boys' Club, across from Tompkins Square Park. It was in the library they had on the second floor which I visited frequently with my growing thirst for language knowledge which was within books. There a Polish- or German-looking white-haired older man sat in a wheelchair, the board in front of him, the pieces scattered throughout. He and the other player were in a pensive trance. Something was happening. I moved closer, felt the artisan concentration of the two players. The librarian saw my interest, asked me if I wanted to learn how to play the game. Of course. Few days later the old man was telling me the names of each of the pieces and how they moved in what he called the war, a battle. My next session with him I only remembered the names of the king and queen and forgot the rest, it had been a full four days and the info had scattered out of my mind, went blank as it got full of street and family life. The rotating and uproar of the speedy streets erasing mental content. Reviewed them all again, after three weeks I was aware of the moves and the names of the pieces, playing with him making the correct movements, never to win but to survive as long as possible. Since then I have always played a cruising game, I taught my son Vitin Ajani in San Francisco when he was about nine, after a few games with him he went on to corner my king each game we played, which is still the case now that he is an adult, I can never trap his king. I have also taught my young cousins in Puerto Rico, Arian y Ariel, and likewise after a few initial games they both now can always defeat my armies on the battle board and paralyze my king. It is puzzling how these sixteen pieces, the pawn-peones peasants the most abundant, the other pieces each repeated twice, the king and the queen who are singular and unique. The game's origins some claim Indian antiquity, some China, India seems like the clearest home. From there it spread to the Persians, early on the Arabs got a hold of it and from the Middle East it took wings with the fervor of Islamic spread through North Africa and on to the Spanish peninsula during the Muslim occupation there. From Muslim Spain it traveled to other European urban centers. The world chess'd out. Some people can design ahead four to five moves; I could never plan beyond two moves. From chess master Bobby Fischer I got the move of bringing the knight out as a first move, next move I push a pawn up two squares and on to the conflict. It is a wonder how those thirty-two pieces can keep one up the night or perhaps even indefinitely till the king is paralyzed. In Cuba José Raúl Capablanca, last name means white cape, developed into a sharp chess player, they called him "la máquina" the machine due to his swiftness in the game; he was also fast with the ladies constantly on tour putting them in checkmate. Nabokov wrote about a chess player in a book called *The Luzhin Defense,* a book I am currently reading. There is Lewis Caroll skipping through boxes of double entendre in *Through the Looking-Glass, and What Alice Found There* where Alice becomes a pawn defending the White Queen. Just the other night reading through Jorge Luis Borges's *Selected Poems* ran across his poem "Ajedrez"

"It was in the East this war took fire.
Today the whole earth is its theater.
Like the game of love, this game goes on forever."
                              Translated by Alastair Reid

For some reason we associate chess with the upper classes, and indeed it was quickly taken as a habit by Persian nobility. In a way it requires a certain amount of leisure-comfort; today the game is everywhere, with the rich and with the poor, United States prisoners practice the game in penal institutions, among them there are some very sharp players. The physical sport closest to chess would be baseball, with its moments of silence, its slow procedure, the importance of the pitcher's aim and psychological shrill as the ball leaves the pitcher's hand to tame the batter with deception, optical illusion. Baseball is a physical sport that is slow, unlike basketball and the frenzy of soccer. During lengthy pauses an outfielder can fall asleep. When I played chess with my cousins Ariel and Arian I always drank a strong cup of café to perk up, since they are young and have spare energy. Their mother Lisa and papa Jorge have taken to chess as well, we had lots of battles within afternoons of sun, splashes of rain showers and nights of coquís singing. The queen defiant, the king posted while the knight horse jumping around with the peasant pawns loose upon the squares of destiny.

Ajedrez

Marble, glass, silver
But mostly wood
The pieces that venture
Out for the kingdom
Maneuvers till you are once
Again in skirmishes surrounded by
Danger,
Crocodiles ready to eat you,
Swords sharp de-neck.
Episodes of medieval attire
Environment it takes you
Back to the game the war
To origins of poetry
Among the warriors,
Europe the Middle East
Epoch medieval
Not so different
Slow division grew.
More similar worlds
Popular people in their
Habitual mess and hardships,
Bread ovens fire
Finger breaks the dough.
Mouth reaching
The curry spice incense
The air, swallow the blend
Dirt moisture atmosphere.
War raging children the women
Are free,
Manitas de Plata Gypsy guitar
His singer in a tune sang:
That woman belong to no one,

"No son de nadie"
Manitas finger popping in the
Back dark,
La dama the queen, woman has the
Most power, Freedom
King just sits throne
Waiting to be cuckold
Cabrón,
Made motionless,
I do not envy nor want his power,
I am satisfied being a peon-peasant
After all if I reach that octave line
I could be transformed into a knight
Or the dama, become woman-queen,
With all that power, I can swing
Lesbo macho across the board
Jumping all possible moves, positions,
Make like a damsel harlot
Red lipstick lip
Sputtering bird whispers,
Watch dinosaurs collapse,
Or toothless old witch
Weaving churning machista
Males like tapetes throwing wood
Into the fire for generations
Bitches aged like Rioja wine
Embroidery of burgundy thread,
Fall into those webs
Submit to green devils
Sitting in the kitchen.
The spider knows what
It weaves: Survival.

Chess has its initial stance
Bravado at commencement
As to turn roosters
Into chickens,
Is it like Puerto Rican dominoes?
Where straw hats and mustaches
Grow caca fear into rivals.
Nothing-la Chucha
It is just ciphers
Pieces fall into hands thru
Chance destiny at grab.
My friend Juan Belen
Once commented upon a group
Of domino players
"They are being antisocial
A way of not dealing with the guest"
Dialogue.
It is also a long stretch of math
Repetitive boredom
Lucky it is spiced with jokes,
Machismo bouquets,
In Cafetíns near jukeboxes
Boleros poetry of tragedy
The dama sublime
Sprays the shuffling passage
Intervals into the sound
Of ivory rectangles
Against wooden table, scratch.

The social of chess for me
Is always memoirs of my son
Vitin-Ajani.
With my young cousins Arian y Ariel,
Watching them excited each

Time they paralyze my king.
I've yet to teach my Moroccan son
The game
Thus there is a chess-full of
Expectations ahead
Schemes-sacrifices
Responsibilities of what
Practical life is,
Taking the game out of the
Zone of jihad
And opening it up to endless
Moves of awareness
Locking the king up
The king is never killed
Assassinated
In the end he is just captured,
Frozen stripped of his powers,
His majesty revives
Like in real vida
He resurrects reincarnates
Once again beside his
Magnificent queen,
In the game of eternal scheme
To obliterate the powerful
Succumb to the harmony of
The plot, submit the power.
Share-scatter the puzzle
Breaking into motion
Piece by peace
Paz
Paseo.

Spanish Language

Primero my Spanish is birth in small mountain town Puerto Rico; it is mother and father, the first bright sunlight of my vocal sounds. But how much Spanish was it, given we were at such a distance from the Iberian Peninsula, an ocean puddle away within climatic metamorphosis, in the Caribbean sprinkled with indigenous Taino words, a mix of vocals from various West African languages. Our Spanish was already the curvy swift mouthing of Andalucía Spanish, the southern bite, along with Canary Island salt which came to the Caribbean in 1492, the same year in the peninsula that Antonio de Nebrija published *Gramática de la lengua castellana.* It was published the same year of the collapse of the last Muslim stronghold of Granada, 1492, thus is a pivotal year for the Spanish language and Latino peoples. I remember as a child my mother would always say to me, "Mira lo que te voy a decir," Look at what I am going to tell you, but she spoke it, do you hear or see language, I conclude finally that the Spanish is intense, images, colors yes. Bright is my view of the movie of my past, when the mountains melted and the buildings surfaced, green became red and gray bricks, it was a sight and it was sound energy. Views of the island linger, recall vivid the rainwater falling huge drops playing timbales upon the newly paved streets. Good portion of our lives we are knocked out in bed like fools curled into an 8 dreaming, remembering, and thinking. What was that dream all about; I carry pictures into the morning café aroma as frames dissolve escaping like vapor. Caribbean language verbose is sun bright light like the days, soundings pierces and comes at you. The Andalucian poet Lorca used the phrase "white milk." What other color could milk be. He does it to throw more fire into the idea of sight, it is not just milk but "white milk," twice the emphasis, so color repeats enlarges becomes more of itself and in another poem "verde que te quiero verde," green that I want you green, green twice thus more green, once is not enough. All the Spanish poets have this color consciousness, this color emphasis, stronger among the Andalusian writers. That is the Spanish that came to our Caribbean island that was the Spanish of my small town, of my family.

As the Spanish poet Pedro Salinas wrote in a small gem of a book, which he wrote while living in Puerto Rico, *Aprecio y defensa del lenguaje,* "El Labrador, el campesino de cualquier pais de vieja civilización habla bien, le gusta hablar bien, admira al que habla bien." Through our Spanish language we are part of that old civilization, our Latin classical connection. The language was for me grandfather the tobacconist in a white suit rolling cigars singing boleros if not listening to a lector read Spanish poetry of the Golden Age. The poignancy-importance of Spanish sight is emphasized by Luis Buñuel and Salvador Dalí when in their film *Un Chien Andalou, A Dog from Andalusia,* they show a barber ready to slice with his sharp shaving razor a beautiful woman's eyes, quickly the scene changes to a goat who gets the razor slash and we behold that creamy goo spilling out. It was a comment Buñuel made on the intensity of the image, seeing, the eye, the visual in our Latino-Spanish-Arábico culture. In our daily life, in our Eros, in our religiosity, in the everyday of poetry. Dalí's paintings are this same perception of memory, a visual remembrance of dreams. Appear. Mira now look at what I am going to tell you, my mother was giving me something which was in the language. Spanish has close to four thousand Arab words which flowered within it. The Arab tongue saw the infancy of the Castilian, the encounter of Latin and Arabic which gave birth to the Spanish language. Thus it is something within it besides vocabulary, cadence perhaps; when I am in Tétouan, Morocco, and listen to people switching from the Arabic to the Spanish it feels like the same language lingo, a continuum of the rhythm cadence, flipped over, force in the two lenguas. Language plays a strong role in our Latino/Arábico communities, what people say carries monumental weight, my uncle José Antonio Hernández, the last of the Aguas Buenas tabaqueros once told me sitting on the balcony of his house, cigars stacked upon his work table next to us, tobacco aroma all around, he said to me something relevant to language, "It is better to get slapped in the face than to have someone talking about you in the vicinity." It was an example of the importance of language in our community. It is like this within the Arabic-Islamic communities as well. Words are hatchet blows, they are fierce like fire. Look at the fate of Salman

Rushdie, the scramble that was caused by his words, I am totally for the freedom of expression of Rushdie, for him to communicate social, spiritual, religious doubt and write it down, it is the role of the writer to question. Yet the affair emphasized the importance of language in the Muslim sphere, that a group of words written down can condemn a person to death. The majority of the Iranian people were against this death sentence (according to a survey taken around the time of the crisis), many claiming that it was opposed to Islamic law in which first there must be a trial on the issue. You would not have known this if you were being informed by American media. Words are the emotions of our relationships. The meaning that guides us, that loves us, divides us, deceives us. In the Spanish language there is a fire, tongue seems to be flinging flames, the Arab is yet much more forceful. Words are the invocation of prayers, the route to spirit. Spain had a cross mixture of ethnicities, the most unlikely European nation of Europe. It is a brew of indigenous Iberian, Roman-Hispano, Celtic, Visigoth, Jewish, Arabic, Berber, and Gypsy. The scholar Robert S. Briffault in the book *The Troubadours,* a text which I have been aware of for decades, talking about the Spanish language, tells us: "when, later, Castile expanded southward the Arabo-Romance vernacular of Andalusia became the foundation of the Castilian tongue." I could read El Quixote of Cervantes which is from the 1600s yet I could not penetrate the Middle English of Geoffrey Chaucer's *The Canterbury Tales* till I found a good contemporary English translation. Spanish developed into maturity and remained on a cruising plateau for centuries. My shaky character is always in English; my major mistakes have been in English. Spanish is the language in which my father gave me direction and firm scoldings. The Spanish language molded a character in me that escapes me in the English, slowly with the passage of years I have dressed the English with my Latin-Español apparel, make the English more respectful, fill it with manners, the protocol of salutation. The warmth, the moisture the colors the force, beat this mischievous English hard, bend it till it screams, set it on fire, cook it, watch it melt into the urgencies of my expression.

Latin Boogaloo

To Francisco Cabanillas

Back in the small town
A child
I used to think there was
A man living under the plaza,
In a subterranean basement.
I used to call him Manolo,
Possible I had sight of him once
Fleeting
Had something in his mouth
Like what is on wine: cork.
Why did I think/imagine?
Schizoid this child play.
I never got to consult my mother
About such such, older, mature.
Wonder
Who else was hearing the voice?
Fiestas patronales,
This one for the dark
Virgin La Montserrat,
Throngs of blue white dresses
Girls, perfume dancing dizzy.
Spinning there la estrella
Ferris wheel
Some ride the Gusano
The worm,
Bigger kids screaming
Every time a cover curtain closed
Over them
Moment blackness,
Watch out the hands

Girls thighs, buttocks,
Ass softure through
The panty nylon-jersey-cotton.

Julio the Bohemio got on
The flying chairs one night,
Cane liquor as if liver.
Till someone said is raining shit
Shit, even on shit shit
A jienda split in sense.
Not even the time of day
Where? Whence?
Take him home
Like a lumber.

The river down we went
Mother Abuela loads of clothes
Bang upon
Rocks with planks of wood,
The village streets
Motion cars, trucks throwing
Cement all over, wooden houses
Disappearing.

Cars that became airplanes
Take off,
Clouds
Landing later upon ice,
No coats winter snow
Traveling hicks,
Become as we entered,
Lucky relatives brought
Warm apparel,
Some Rican relative

With a 50s Packard
Look like a giant frog.
First thing for me
Entering building was smell
Cold cement iron
Marble stairs
Climbing like zigzag
Long halls pasillo paseo,
To Apartment house-home
Novo Bohío tis was,
Open door
There quick kitchen
Sink, bathtub
Scope first time.
Railroad flat.

Americanos whosit
Them
Start calling us the Spanish
Like we language sound
Not bone-meat.

Bizarre mestizos
Drop into blender
Moving buildings, streets
Windows rotating
Lengua licking
Bricks the savannah birds
Frozen in the past,
Because now accent in both
Languages, both are on loan to me,
Pictures climb up
A division
Thoughts of nothing?

Nothing created nothing.
El boogaloo dancing between
Walls the new vocals
To understand lips
Fast machine tongue spit,
STOP
Slow down
Grind it up bone tight,
Park visuelos window
Vasitos de colores,
With the syllabic injuries
Make suns in semi blue
Skies.
One time Bronx
With the language of Cervantes
Trying to make sense
Of all the nothing that
Everything became,
Bringing it back to focus,
Latin Manhattan
Like Virgil war stories,
Bickering family,
Uncle threw a knife slash
At own shadow,
The way they lost Andalusia
The Moros endaggaring
One to the other
Petit arguments,
They were overtaken by two cousins
Having sex.

Package of baggage,
Like Checo once said
In the Cantina

When he migrated to New York
In a job interview Porican asked
him if he
Knew how to "empaquetar,"
And he had to pause before answer,
Since in Puerto Rican
"Empaquetar" could mean swindling
Deceit as if in lying,
But he got through the double
Entendre duplex triplex
Sound waves of meaning,
Later out tenement window
Down the street with 3 p.m. café
Eye peeling
Sipping the past as the present
Sugar dissolves Sonia appears
And Carmen's far corner curves
Like walking question marks ??
Upon the street venture
Caffeine retina scoping joking
As life is a vacilón,
Ah sí la cojo.

In Manhattan the Spanish and
English underground
Half city is in el tren way sub
The number 6 Lexington
Spent my youth in motion
Lower East Side/East Harlem
Vaivén yo-yo
La Marketa fruits and Tropical
Vegetables, panas, ñame, yautia
Speechless objects what could
Translate taste like.

The 6 to the Bronx Music Palace
Hunts Point learning how to
Read maraca seeds shaking in
The sonneteers palms,
Accents smeared like lipstick
Red the line of the lips
Crossed like a border.
New York Ricans chopped the
Cuban Son up,
Out of clave momentarily,
Put English lyrics
For the now generation,
Project verbose,
Fast chops of James Brown
Southern orange soda,
Saintly kitsch orange camisas,
A vamp stomp to stop your heart
Charge
Timbale chops like
Knives slicing air,
Jump
Trombones in unison
A quake like the South Bronx
Wanna fall down collapse.

Mambo melts Flamenco foot
With Yoruba circles
Searching for Orishas,
Step point of shoe,
Move shake shoulders
Like itches trembling,
Legs scissor spread rápido,
The waist bring her to you: inject.
Dancing is flirt mating motions,

Spin she he he she to
Together marking clave time,
Rhythm nucleus follow
Melody expresses contradiction,
The three/two time watch
Above changes to the side
Behind us now seems,
Melody goes everywhere,
But the clock of the clave
Always there
Riding out the chaos grounds you

Links like a chain
Circle sky forever
Loops of beat
Stars are scattered maraca seeds,
Gyrating brings you back
To the button,
Cuchy cuchy cuchi ka
There it is
It is there
There is   it
Is   there
Where
COMO
Ahí no mah.
Language immense greater
Than nationality,
No country politic
Plenty culture song dance
Libre,
Which are turfs savannahs

Mountains for son Montunos
Bahías, boulders trees
Nations (Notions) if you can,
Sentiment of the sounds
We are,
The melancholy of speech
Pity Mountains, ay bendito
Campanas of labia,
The fire of moisture tongues
Combined in new words
Wor(l)ds
Taino de Amazona
Fresh touch of desire,
Guanayamao my jaw of native pala
Chewing tobacco y España
Golden Age poetry-lyrics,
Spit them out or
Essential Romanic tongue
Spillage like
Scribbles discord as the Arab
Is a scimitar razor sharp
Put-downs of hard remembrance
Tongues as long as the desert,
Talk word supremacy
Chismological communities:
Singular your mama.

No modernity erases my peasant side
It came in through language
Hardened with my bones
Invisible if wants
Rock hard agitation
Jump for your lump
The tongue is salt and fire

As the flute sounds of Eros desire,
Clicks to the clit,
Gutsy y brash-clash
Off like tumbadora slaps.

Avoidance/around the bush
Is for brainy American English,
I paint red the sky
Speak out gut-balls –cock
Pingus is
I am Severo, like my father,
Who drank an ocean of insults,
Till he vomited the world out
Carrying it upon his back
Painted me and my sister
In the mountain world of
"Gente baja" what was all about
Pueblo folk forever printed,
They all made it to the church
To the word of God,
Meant what he meant
Severo focused upon malicious intent,
Told me not to pity the pitiful
They are god's necessity,
Pawns in destiny's hand
Selves better blind
Sun's light would explode retinas,
Purpose they have enough fulfillments.
Generosity is a symptom of the poor,
Work and do harm to no one,
Don't ask anyone for nothing
Don't give them anything either.
Stay home watch *Wheel of Fortune*
Not a centime wasted,

Allah is the one who proportions
Severo was my father
he was never my friend.

As a kid with Papa
We went over words
In Spanish-English dictionary
Wrote meanings down
Pronunciation.
Anticipating future life
As translator,
Upon the fence balance,
The border crossings,
A playground of syllables
Jumped as kid with
"Papo Got His Gun"
Shooting with words,
Orthography upside down
slamming off the bricks.
It was the morning of a long day.
From the island in Spanish
News of Albizu Campos dying
Radiation torture that in jail,
Governor ex-poet put him in.
And that / that those are the Christians,
Figúrate tú,
The devil on the phone is one thing,
But comes to your door is another,
Chew on that orange
While I peel you a fresh.

My mother erased Manhattan
Skyline
By bringing me up on

The proverbs of the Spanish,
Staring out window Chrysler building
Holding maracas
Doing the boogaloo
While I chew on octopus salad
Next to red beans and plantains,
Where is dónde está?
What choice do I have
When I drink Tamarindo juice
In the Manhattan Latin mountains
Of Guayococobonex, floor six
No elevator,
What you left something up there
Six below zero snow on the street
No reruns, Forget about it.
We were Prisoners of Spain
Prisoners of the Americans.
Once I heard voices as a child
Under the cement of the plaza,
It was the voice of Manolo,
It had an echo from Andalusia,
To the mountain town
I can't go back there.
What the lengua gave me
Is still the echo inside
Silence chamber shadow of the guitar.
Where resides my shame*
Shining through vasitos
De colores.
Gaze at what I have told you
words are color, sound.
Language not heard but seen/
MIRA!
*read: verguenza, character

134

Sueños

The real is I get tired night body rest must. Reading lifelong habit to get my imagination to dance, eves to get my eyes tired for sleep, yet always the toss and turn, I toss more than a lump of shit in water before stumbling into the depth covacha of sleep, sleep is not always sueño, the body the figure thrown rolled into the figure 8 position into a pair of pliers legs arms reaching. Motion forward mattress turns into a snake, a woman, a fruit, are we moving, boat? Something is in motion; half-conscious mind struggles to recall the drama. Something starts to happen, becomes blank, black, gone, a hole. You depart; down it goes, so go to it. A film rolls, chasing being chased, view out of a window, what city, where is this geography? Am I kissing a tree, guayacán, roble, guayaba bushel? The young fine girl next door? What is in my hands, hands, who in am. The episodes lose themselves, disfigure. Smoke. What was that? Episodes of dreams become vapor when the morning sun rises, struggle with black café to recollect. Scattered pictures, photos hanging on to the caffeine walls. Something remembered the mind pushes back toward the azabache of the nocturnal frames, back into itself, scatters, things break up, Manhattan buildings blossom at the tips of tropical mountains, geography topsy-turvy, inside out, upside down, chronology forgets itself, melts. Simultaneously the dream presents everything at once. A cubist painting blows up, fragments fall, red roses stars in light blue sky. Juan Gris adjacent the bottle of red wine, the clock melted, or Dalí in the *The Persistence of Memory,* my interior drops down a ravine, blue river rocks midst vapor, frogs bamboo dance river waving hairy bush, jump flight of white garzas over the landscape. Giant butterflies with Miró designs flapping wings as I hear maraca güiro scratch. Toward the future scenarios I am repetitions, but mostly my dreams are visitations perhaps of past lives, jinn's chance waving through the air. We must be other people simultaneously. I have dreams which have nothing to do with me, which never become part of my future, having nothing to do with my past, dreams must be a present now phenomena reeling, maybe if we run camera while we are out sleeping-dreaming thrown comatose zombie like who knows what scenarios would come into focus what if we apprehend "gaunt night creatures" around our bed, like H. P. Lovecraft claimed creatures of his night horrors, supposedly they were thin, like thread in motion, horns they had, thus cabrones, part goats, who knows what infestations declare themselves while we are mineral. Ghouls from the Arab world cemetery-Makbara, thieves, who swallow people and take on the appearance of what they just imbibe, all over town we see them, talk to them, watch them maneuver, they look real, so are your dreams. For Black Elk they spoke history and mapped his stance in geography almost all native traditions have a link with dreams, bring them out to dance in the bright sunlight, footsteps spell the words that an eagle expressed to them. Ghouls were semblances in *The Arabian Nights.* In my mestizo Caribbean psyche Taino Opias float about by the periphery of rivers, circle of the yucayeque recall a habitat of insects and lizards, alacranes, flying roaches, frogs, owls shrieking, images that print out at night. Opias, Taino spirits, lizard-alligator texture flesh. The movie I see in dreams feels as if looking down into a well, a cave, something round, now below, eventually above, scenario not happening within us but at a distance from where we are comatose observers, the rest of that mambo simulcast, must be all a contradiction. I could never sleep with my belly button facing up, the navel entrance I have to cover it other-wise eye voyage through phantasmagoria, nightmares, screams, shock-ing appearances, fear pesadillas. In Morocco they put pillows and cover mantas out into the morning sun and air as if to cleanse the night out of them. Milan Kundura said *Life Is Elsewhere.*

WHO/WHAT/WHERE

San Francisco asleep
Un moment
Taino village sparks
Women girls all naked,
A river cruising upon canoas,
One toss in bed the scenery
Changes to New York
The roof staring at a kite
Some kid displaced there,
To the left of the screen
Pigeons in cages,
Later in time
Sunlight peeping
Through my window,
Composing self the something,
Whatever it is,
Morning gathering the noche
Fragments scattered into
An 8 eight becoming One-1-
Becoming persona again.
Café desiring as habitual
Junky looking for the flavor.
Aromatic "Baghdad by the Bay"
Herb Caen would say.
See only a sky
The city wind drifts,
Mexican Ranchera music
Window house nearby,
Awake in the Mission District
San Francisco, Califas
Más Northern Mexico summit.
Not far original church

San Francisco de Asis
Misión Dolores,
History claims a creek
Even a lake wide water
Ran nearby—
Gone today.
Somewhere progress
Filled up gutter street houses
Atop in the future.
Where is James Stewart
Looking for Carlotta Valdes
Through the streets of
Mentality in the film
Vertigo de Alfred Hitchcock?
1958 was a place,
Pachucos somewhere in the hood
Big old Buicks y Chevrolets
Sculptured hair like the façade of Pontiacs
Battleships glued with Halka pomade
Throwing shadow onto forehead.
Now, Frisco inside
Of North African night daze
As also,
I present the Caribbean into
The picture by throwing on
Tito Puente cha cha chas
Along with café con leche
Pan dulces from La Victoria
Panadería on 24th Street,
That apartment of charm hangs in
My dreams an evermore
No matter the Geo
Alights that long hallway
Painted light turquoise,

Woman Elisa Ivette head
Hair black aceituna skin
Olive Taina whispers
Caribbean. Children toddlers
Bunk beds,
Mission High School
Around the corner
Structure architecture Morisco past present,
Now sprinkled with
Central American spice Spanish
The street.
That epoch continues dreaming.

Drinking books by window
Skylight, lost in magic words.
Sunken the night
The curve of her flesh
Against the pillow.
New York that turns tropical river.
The eyelid opens closes the curtain,
Inside appearance
Breathing with my thoughts,
My mother appears,
We are walking together
Back in the town
Her yellow dress
The bright light of the Caribe day,
Scene always like golden negative.
Bed was by it and sleeping
Took a walk into the wall
Nada I came back with
A bag full of nothing.

Waking the trail to school
Mists, bricks lingering.

Out the window tenement paintings
Cold gris colores.
What is this?
My mother spoke in her dreams,
Once I answered her
Thought we were in conversation
Till sister Gladys rang
"She is asleep, stupid."
Grandmother came to visit
From the island
Father's mother
Afro-Taina look with long white
Hair
Few times she sat up middle
Of dark nowhere
Calling out "espíritu, píritu, espíritu"
Scare me tremble as she
Used to see things awake,
Imagine asleep.

Dream I was a lizard
Brushing through rocks
Feet slip making
Güiro scratch sound as
Shuffle through the mineral,
Arrive into yucayeque,
Take position scope Areyto dance
In round circle
Walk-dance the moon
Cold blood of my skin
As I hang on to a moon crater

Upside down
Staring toward vast black,
Green blue nickel
The earth
At the bottom pit obscurity
Green light tone. Va pa'llá.

Wake up North Africa Norte
Minaret call to prayer
Perfume de Café,
Almond scent
Rose water sprinkles.
I inquire of the almuad,
Interview my pillow
But the pillow is just as
Lost and wet.

Calls out to me:
Where
When
What
Who?

The Costumes of Peasant Folk

It has always fascinated me to see the peasant dress and designs of folk from different parts of the world. There is something in the style, patterns, and colors that seems to match one with the other, as if pre-industrial communities had an invisible link or unity, no matter the what of the distances. Look at Eastern European folk dress; compare them to the Guatemalan, Welsh, to an indigenous Peruvian, or Berber rug patterns to Navajo, do they share geometry, illuminated kinship despite wide oceans and mountains. Taos Pueblo-Navajo to Buddhist designs, sand painting, clothing patterns, beads. The world was larger and more apart, yet melded more together. As the local was so particular, each individual, each similarity to collective universes, as everywhere the same difference. Skin upon earth soil, stars, moon which we look up to, who owns the sky? Yet within this age of electronics and the internet, we are getting smaller, condensed. Kitschy minor craftsmanship all around us. The quality of craft has suffered. The dancing, the music seems to become each day more "foreign," less natural. Less detail, look what has happened to the cha-cha-cha, Rumba, plena, Bomba, guaguancó, son montuno all now swept under the umbrella of Salsa, I need and like those hues of old, the texture of the full panorama, now a-days there is no elaboration, it's like a lack of concentration. The attitude to life, hard work, discipline, and children is diffused by this modern urge toward a notion of freedom that is artificial. There is nothing but responsibility in life. That's the freedom—the choice—you have, to achieve your responsibilities to self and family, to community. Unequal, we are as differences united in the same, analogous air. Vive la différence! The most beautiful thing of being upon this earthiness is precisely the differences; the human species is one, yes divided into different ethnicities, geographic regions, skin colors, tones, tunes if you may, hair textures, human features, the beautiful quilt of the human race. We are poly rhythms and poly colors. Thrown upon this earth which is not round, empty the sphere of its water and tell me that it was not the nervous hands of Salvador Dalí who designed it. We live this beautiful yin con yang, oppositoriness, male-female. What makes this music of

African drum mixed with the Spanish guitar (which is also Arabic La'ud) so immense this cultura of various classical threads concentrated embroidery, the mulata has it all, the mestizaje she wears, she is the queen of paradise. A culture that incorporates. Space and weight the only equality. Creatures have the limitations of their own form, live within them or derail and suffer the consequences of going against natura. Individual beings can be made aware of a direction but it is up to them to perceive and to have the power to go, create. People seem to grow into destinies to become selves that were already planted within. The sweetness of the mango is in the seed. We are from within, out. No matter what the life examples, individuals go play what is within, they play-sing-become what they came here with. "If you were born to be a hammer, from the heavens will rain the nails" Rubén Blades reminds us in a Salsa tune.

The Peasant, the campesino love stories and the recitation of popular poetry is their domain, they are oral fragrance, they are the beads of an immense necklace, with the home remedies, cooking food with an elevated patience, slow food they uphold a cherished treasure, they are also courteous and respectful. You enter a small bar in Puerto Rico known as cafetín, you shake everyone's hands, the lawyer, the singer, the school teacher, the mendicant, the disabled, you salute all beings present, I have noticed this protocol in the Moroccan cities of my dwelling amongst the people, as they were once in Andalucía, the refrain "mi casa es su casa" is an old Arabic proverb which passed to us via the Spanish language. The campo folk practice order and calm and are conservative, not in the North American political sense of the word but as a manifestation of the order of nature, upholding traditions as in the culture of the singing of the décima. Complex rhyming scheme within the simplicity of the campesino memory.

The Turks, the Indians, the Mesoamericans, the Caribbeans, Incas, Aztecas, Eastern Europeans, Tibetans, Chinese, Hungarians, Polish, Czechoslovakians, Guatemalans, Peruvians, Ecuadorians, Germans, Albanians, all seem to be locked up in a Bashō Renga Haiku upon a long winter road, cold as cold as hot ice infinity. The Earth. Snow Pampas,

Cordilleras, Andes, Atlas Mountains, Siberia of ice cubes, frozen skeletal trees swaying in the icy mental mist. Or hot tropicality so delicious by the Caribbean Sea, pours more open sea salt atmosphere through the coast bouncy and effervescent más you float, levitate. Dance waves simulations of Yoruba fertility, Shango chasing Oshun or one of his other women of water waves. Yemayá. Wave line of cocks gyrating back and forward to the corresponding sea of pussy shells, mass recollection of planetary memory. I go with mountain girl any moment, away from city (urban) university.

Fresqueria or Eros is what makes us human. Imagine cats that just jump the female in constant violation. Education más bien. Character is the natural, practical sign of the oral classic refinement, sharp spice, los troubadours of everywhere, the storytelling memoirs epic process of tradition, folk loom is universal knowledge, of manners, of respect, humbleness. Flirting, rapping, flores are the necessary fore-poetry of life, play the spell of love. The classical art of tradición. The mountain kisses are nervous and send shock revelations spine down toward pisa pie, where you do not miss the foot nor the step, as moist tongues sing together. Jíbara dresses dancing Mapeyé. The world is the same dress yet false knowledge has come in to divide us. Attempts to iron smooth the wrinkled lines, the wild curvy spontaneous reality of the world's geographic robe. Artificial forces attempt to iron out smooth with false knowledge to divide with myths of race. Despite the fast digital-age efforts to smooth the world's curvy bumpy spontaneous reality. The beautiful differences prevail, as such the colors and shapes sancocho unite, not multi-cultures which implies separateness but FUSION culture united in weavings of impossible sameness, in disparity clapping hands while lifting the vast florid dress. Of the Worldrobe concert.

Future Mountain

The literate fuss makes such
Day long one once gone come
Or going what on earth.
The question is is or not.
And send and bring. Till.
Rope knots listen to the flute
You snakes.

The Polka steps in the tropics
Away from Bohemia/Central Europe
Jevas lift the orange dresses
Above the knees.
A mass Polka of Chicanos
In Watsonville
Whispers of Slovenia/
Hungarian rise
Civilization harbored in the eyes
Follow the hands
The swift of turn's body motion,
Menudo soup
Croatia my foot.
The agriculture smiles at harvest
Fest of Strawberries dancing,
Manzana not the apple city
But Latin American plaza north way,
What eye have seen upon
Journey from Toledo to Toboso,
From Guatemala to Guatepeor
From Salva truch to Bernal Heights,
O give me those hands that folded,
Lifted dress previous to her squat,
San Fransa Nicoyala.

Horchata de Cacao dulce.
Chocolat chocante.

Dulcinea the sweet embarrassed
The lust behind the shame,
Covered in veil Sunday road
To Church—as well the Mosque
Friday the same path.
Mazurka Polaca is the preindustrial
Barley.
Jíbaros-Guajiros Guachos-peones
Rise early as in the game of chess
Peasants-peones first to move,
Water on face in darkness
Antes the coocurucu of the roosters,
Cool morning no matter the
Inferno afternoon drops into serenity,
Mist dwells montunos arboreal
Trees inhale neblina looks tobacco smoke.
Café negro within once lata de Campbell
Soup gone
Opened in perfect rim,
No cut lip
Cured with the black liquid.
The Tobacco workers march
To the chin-chall
White straw sombreros illuminating
Through birth of nascent light.

The Middle East cities
Europe a semblance-closer
Middle Ages
In tempo, street grid,
Place of worship

Artisans of task
The wide space between
Societies spread later.
Vegetables meat scarce,
Asia stirred vegetables
With salty sauce,
Bamboo shoots
Celery vines
Cabbage.
Get out the way of
China man carrying Cabbage,
Don't chabbage with cabbage,
Leaves headed toward the wok,
Oil Sesame,
Peasant rural communism
Works like a before Marx ideogram,
Him talking about what we
Nature assembles grows like weed,
Plantación adentro camarada,
Who were the first towners,
That lined up footage toward
The city,
Disappear the desert
Left to the flavor on the outskirts,
Water
Egyptians Heliopolis
The books were the buildings of
Alexandria,
Mexico City floating islands
Population in the millions
Before the Spanish.
Peruvians enclosed in stone,
Sipping coca té eating
Red beans and Potatoes,

Jumping mountains with Llamas
Gone in red caps blue skirt women
Vanish sky top levels of Machu Picchu.

In all Europe work land
Belong to landlords
(How did they obtain the turf)
The swindlers up late,
The workers rise antes sun,
Use the land for your needs,
Sons of whores
If I sell it I sell you too
And your mama,
Send me your daughter
When she is sixteen,
If the chick has an egg
Bring it up with the songs
Next to the peons
The hand clapping
Add to the cousins.

The Hacienda announces
Harvest of Café Feast,
The muchedumbre spills
Onto open fields
With steps of dance
Like rain falling,
Alegre grins
White pants, las Marías
With red blouses
"... con su pollera colorah
Mírala cómo viene
Mírala cómo vah ..."
Shine moon fire water

Pitorro, the feast starts
With one güiro scratch
Terminates when people faint,
Dance flirtation
Inspires procreation
Crowd the mountains
More mocoso creatures,
Soon they gotta funche eat,
Meat captured sheep, goats,
In the Sahara you eat the stars,
The stars are your books,
Read horizon light line,
Search through the heavy mantas
For your wife's leg
Conjunto ruffle of chingalín
Accompanies
Camel snores.

Saw once rural Holland
Persona full of cream Gouda
Colossal Shoes of wood
Look like two boats,
Amaze at pack of crazy moderns
Speaking what lunacy,
The circus has arrived he thought
The earth
Scoping excited brash appearances
Out of place like books
In an illiterate world.

A mango in Alaska,
Cuckaroaches invade
A dance of chickens.
The lyrics

Of the Boleros.
The pages of the books.
In the age of pure
Classic gold.
Destiny mountain girl
Save me a dance

In all other be.
Wait the tree, the shadow.
Under.

Latin American Dance

People dance the harvest; people dance the moon, humanity dances cock songs in flower marriage, dances new birth. Dance spirits cometh and goeth. Sun fire steps with the flower fertile hydro furnace womb, creation. They dance circle round they dance parallel lines of male-females. Back and forth in and out. Rain dance the natives keep the earth producing barley, corn, yucca, potatoes. Taino Areyto was música dance circle and song-chant of the tribal memory the whole village partakes. The Opias and Cemis possess into the night, Tobacco aroma links, inter-realms of green light entities. Fly feather. Folks dance the wedding, they dance the baptism. As a whole the Caribbean mixture dances, with Spanish Flamenco blood with African sway, no one stays sitting down. Cuba has been the origin of many of the Latin American dances, danzón, cha cha cha, mambo, bolero, la Pachanga, in the case of the Pachanga, which was the rhythm of the Cuban revolution, it came in simultaneously with the bearded revolutionaries, both entering Havana in 1959. Was it Fajardo, the Cuban flute player, who brought the rhythm to New York around this time? The Puerto Ricans in the clubs of the Bronx defined the dance steps to it. Johnny Pacheco the Dominican New Yorker helped to establish the Pachanga rhythm in the City of Latin Dance. The Pachanga was a mix of Son Montuno with Merengue. Some hear the Mambo swifts along with the Colombian cumbia. The Pachanga spread like a fire in a dry forest. On the Lower East Side Puerto Ricans in a pachanga party tumbled a building wall down, the old worn bricks blasted out with the rhythm obeying the law of gravity, a whole wall stack of bricks thus exposing a living room painted pink fell onto a vacant lot below. Poricans ate the stairs evacuating, as the next obvious thought was that the whole building was going to collapse.

Cuba is the Rumba of dance and voice-song, steps pure hips, total torso involved, gyrating mating coquet between male and female. Similar would be the Puerto Rican Bomba dance, a circle the drums, maracas, sonero-singer chorus-call and respond. In the Bomba the dancer directs the drummers, the primo or subidor the sharp tone drum beckons the feet. It is the most African manifestation on the island, roots back to the Congo, some of the other Caribbean islands have similar rhythm/dances. Arguments abound as to the origin of the Bomba; some point toward the area of Mayagüez on the west coast of the island; others claim Loíza Aldea in the northeastern coast. The Bomba drums once were made from empty barriles of rum or bacalao in the region of Ponce, they have a style of playing where they lay the drums down horizontal as if to feel the vibrations of the earth, capture the sonic-spell from the Caribbean waves nearby. Whichever region gave it birth it is an important Afro-Puerto Rican development based direct upon African rhythms. In its dance motions you can also detect the Spanish gypsy Flamenco. It has various styles or tempos, the "Sica," the "Yuba," the "Holandes," all feature the dancer directing the beats of the drummers, especially the Primo of sharp tone timbre chasing the hips, shoulders and waist and hand movements of the dancers. The crowd joins in on the chorus and entering and departing from the Bomba dance circle at will. Other African descendent peoples of Latin America have similar dances. San Basilio de Palenque, Colombia, has a similar dance tradition. It is also one of the first free communities of Africans in the Western hemisphere. They maintain a language of Congolese vocals mixed with Portuguese within a dialogue uniquely their own. The Puerto Rican Bomba has been taken by island immigrants to Manhattan to Chicago. Ponce city on the Caribbean coast is definitely the origin of the Plena, another dance-song rhythm. Plena lyrics are based on everyday events; in the 50s a radio station on the island did the news in Plena fashion.

The Cuban Rumba has three main styles the Yambü, the Guaguancó, the Columbia, all feature drumming, singsong sonero with chorus response. The Rumba is also of the Spanish Gypsies and was given African flavor in the Caribbean. All peoples dance, have agriculture and gather to celebrate its fruits. The Berbers, ginger color tribe of Africa, have a back and forward drama, row of men row of women, the women are big mamas but move ass buttocks with such delightful facility, they appear like the round belly clay sculptures of Miró activated in jelly movements. They play hand drums, that are similar to the panderetas of the

Plena, a favorite Berber percussive drum, most likely that is the origin of the Plena panderos, must've slipped into Spain during the Morisco occupation and come to the Caribbean with the subsequent waves of peoples migrating. Other North African drums are shaped like hourglasses. They are miniature and make sharp sounds.

In Cuba the "Guateque" formed. Father de Las Casas saw it and described it as a dance similar to one performed by the workers of Andalucía. It also had a singer and a chorus. The word *guateque* grew in the popular sphere to mean dance, party, usually out of the city in the campos.

Dancing was my youth-teen 'hood in New York of the mid 60s. There was a dance almost every day somewhere in the city, the Bronx, Brooklyn, Manhattan. I was too young to have made it to the legendary Palladium Club, but I knew elders who used to go party-dance there and looking at their eyes I knew there was something electric, excitement special on that dance floor. Once visiting a friend, his older sister was getting dressed to go to the Palladium, while the phonograph all the time spun Machito tunes. She prepared herself. Her name was Sonia and a girlfriend of hers she called Letty (or something like that, Tetty, Seddy, Litty qué sé yo) came to the door. She was all ready in a beautiful light-blue dress, nylon stockings with that black line in the back, where the batata ran. She and Sonia were gorgeous. I was wishing I was older and knew better how to dance, I knew they would disappear into the lights of the metropolis, to a place of laughter and dance and the music of the magic, Palladium, it was known as the home of the Mambo, for the excellence and enthusiasm of its dancers; from there it spread to the whole country. The Palladium ambiance did what the Latino-Caribbean had done from jump; they integrated all the colors, peoples of all ethnicities would go there, it was all based on one thing: dance, rhythm a trait that runs through all human flesh. Already in 1949 New Yorkers were in there dancing, throwing scissor-chopping motions with elbows and legs. The rest of the country was suffering from segregation. Latinos became the overwhelming mofongo pulp in the club. Puerto Ricans from Spanish Harlem came down, it was a train hop take the 6 Lexington down to Grand Central take the west Broadway line up a stop and there you were. It cost 75 cents to get into the club; remember it was the late 40s, early 50s, the subway ride was a dime. The Palladium Club this época was drawing big celebrities such as Marlon Brando, who would jump on stage and touch-play caress the Congas. Oh yeah, Frank Sinatra went there to listen to his Latino counterpart in Tito Rodríguez when the bandleader sang boleros. Tito was also a swinging sonero of mambos and cha cha chas. The Palladium had a broad appeal amongst the hipsters, beatniks, jazz musicians, Italians, and Jews were regular dancers on the floor. The musicians Duke Ellington, Count Basie were spotted listening to the Mambo beats. The singers Billie Holiday and Ella Fitzgerald perfect splendors spotted in the stylish and glamorous dance hall at 53rd and Broadway. Everyone dressed to kill in suits and ties, proper shoes well shined, with handkerchiefs in pockets or in the hands. Women with kan-kan flares, ruffles, gowns, fancy purses. Wayne Shorter arrived and was inspired to create a tune called "Palladium" with his group Weather Report. The Palladium was the New York world of elegance. It was the pearl of the New York elegante Puerto Rican-Latino world.

Pedro "Cuban Pete" Aguilar was a New York Puerto Rican whose family had taken the trip across the ocean way before the mass Puerto Rican exodus of the late 40s and early 50s. Perhaps they came on the famous *Marine Tiger* ship which made so many trips during the San Juan to New York migratory wave, Marintaya full of Jíbaros, chickens in boxes, guitars in arms, folks singing serenading the Atlantic waves, first stop near the Brooklyn Navy Yard thus Williamsburg the first Puerto Rican community in New York. Pedro "Cuban Pete" Aguilar tried his hand at boxing, till one day the Cuban singer Miguelito Valdés, who had been an amateur boxer himself as well in his native Cuba, where he was born from a Cuban father and a Mexican Yucatec mother, had seen the young man dancing and advised him to join a dance competition. Pedro did, and he won $1,000. Wow, in the early 50s if $1,000 dollars fell upon you, you had some pasta. The young man turned his attention and his discipline from the boxing ring onto the dance floor. It was at the Palladium where this human charge of electricity broke out and people paid attention. He scribbled with his legs, at times doing something approximate lindy hop, Charleston, mixing the Caribbean with nitty-gritty Savoy Ballroom steps, melting the tribes together, paying homage to the Clave beat of the Mambo, to Africa, mother culture of us all. He twisted and went into contortions, squatting and jumping, walking like a chicken, hopping like a kangaroo, he trembled, tumbled, and turned himself inside out, he danced within the clave, that is he followed the beat of the drum not the melody which is the secret of all true Latin dancers. Stay attentive to the discussion that the tumbadora (conga) is having with the bongos and the maracas. Merge into the groove known as the martillito (the hammer) and throw your bone structure into it. It was in the Palladium that Pedro met the New York Italian girl named Millie Donay and they danced a love calligraphy around each other, loops and spins that took them all the way to the altar. Together on the floor of the Palladium they sizzled, defined timing and coordination. A choreographic harmony in body language that very few people have been able to achieve since. The Mambo from Cuba, the dance machine of the Americas, hit New York. Forget about it! The Palladium was the home of the Mambo; I am eternally frustrated at time and space for my age was that of a minor when all this fire was burning in New York. The Palladium had opened its doors in 1947 and the final curtain dropped in 1966.

Then the dancers moved to the Corso Club on 86th St. and over to the Colgate Gardens, that eventually became the Cheetah Club. Simultaneously with the Palladium, there was the old El Club Caborrojeño, the Happy Hills Casino, and the Park Palace in Spanish Harlem. But nothing compared with the nuclear adrenaline of the Palladium. In New York the Afro-American and Puerto Rican communities were one big dance party of the generations. It eventually continued with doo-wop and into Hip-Hop right out of the Afro-American-Rican Bronx. Afro Latino harvest dance of the imagination. With Ray Barretto I too sing, "¡Que Viva la Música!" Baila conmigo. Dance with me Mambo At:

La Pachanga

To the memory of Pedro "Cuban Pete" Aguilar

Fandango, Waltz, Contradense,
Mapeyé,
Was the mountain
Nothing was excluded
No one sat down.
Marineros naves
Anchors deep in the sand.
They practice vocabulary
And they taught nasty words
Within novo tropic nights,
While tongues filled
With succulent pineapple,
Calabaza bowl of stew iguana
Cassava bread
Trapped in back molars
Nothing left
But to precipice down throat
In the oven ferment into shit
New innovation compost
Intercontinental manure
Spilling original bowels.

Tonight is the "Jarana"
En casa de Juja
Por la carretera toward
The mamey trees.

After Caguitas
Rise levels of trees,

Of mountain goats,
Horses charros
Road of Yucatán
Potros arrive Jarana
And paso fino a la Waltz.
Mexicanao strut
Chili foot tongue
Heel-toe toe heel
Head side to side
Spin
Left right electric
Skirts circle waves
Chili of desire
What's more Danzón than
Veracruz
Caramel draped in white gauze
Lobsters hidden under
The skirts
Yuca invites sea swells
The palm trees droop
As if bowing
Under the half moon,
Guitars corner of Dolores
Avenue of Pain,
Jump into the dance
Drums push you
What choice does one have?
Life is hunger, desire,
Licking verbs,
Somehow you heard the call of flesh,
Stomp away the Joropo,
Colombia y Venezuela
Joropo dancers leg scramble

Foot stomping as if
Shaking off roaches,
A pushing a shoving,
In the spin mozorbete
Hands all over the biscocho,
Mestizas of skinny legs
Carrying mountain buttocks,
Swishing
Mouths of sweet Chiclets,
Later zarapes thrown near
Guayaba bushels
Puzzling the saltine sweet sabor
Mexico
Birth of the nation
Chile pulse on corn
Forward Jarabe Tapatío
Guadalajara plazas of smoke
Asian eyes of la China Poblana
Sass of youth breast still pointed
Lift through the peasant blouse,
The fibers of the zarape
Fire might as well be.
Suffer the retina pain
Next day chopped up
Gathering splinters
Recuperate with goat soup
Tortillas maíz
Jalapeño awareness.

Gentleman in Puerto Rico
Wanting to be more Spanish
Than an olive
Swore Grandparents danced

La Jota,
Which fact is that it is of Moorish
Origin
Thus Jota on Jotos
The more you go
The more you come back.

Mapeyé-like a rush
Jíbaro mountains
People dance like chickens
And like guineas the chicken
Ave from Africa
It chirps squabbles and
Runs in a nervous jitter.

The Pachanga starts
At the first güiro scratch
And doesn't stop till people faint
Marías Carmens Nildas
Of Nadias
Have been known to jump
Out of windows
Already dancing through
The infinite air of
Either ether or ether eit.
Gone. Scrambling
Towards la pachanga,
Towards la chingada
Se las llevo la fregada
The washing has taken them,
The clave put them in the whirlpool,
It don't stop till there are children
Born

And it all repeats:
Tun tun tun tún
Tun tun tun tún
Tun tun tun tún.

LITERATURE
is not the same thing as
PUBLISHING

Coffee House Press began as a small letterpress operation in 1972 and has grown into an internationally renowned nonprofit publisher of literary fiction, essay, poetry, and other work that doesn't fit neatly into genre categories.

Coffee House is both a publisher and an arts organization. Through our *Books in Action* program and publications, we've become interdisciplinary collaborators and incubators for new work and audience experiences. Our vision for the future is one where a publisher is a catalyst and connector.

Funder Acknowledgments

Coffee House Press is an internationally renowned independent book publisher and arts nonprofit based in Minneapolis, MN; through its literary publications and Books in Action program, Coffee House acts as a catalyst and connector— between authors and readers, ideas and resources, creativity and community, inspiration and action.

Coffee House Press books are made possible through the generous support of grants and donations from corporations, state and federal grant programs, family foundations, and the many individuals who believe in the transformational power of literature. This activity is made possible by the voters of Minnesota through a Minnesota State Arts Board Operating Support grant, thanks to the legislative appropriation from the arts and cultural heritage fund. Coffee House also receives major operating support from the Amazon Literary Partnership, the Jerome Foundation, The McKnight Foundation, Target Foundation, and the National Endowment for the Arts (NEA). To find out more about how NEA grants impact individuals and communities, visit www.arts.gov.

Coffee House Press receives additional support from the Elmer L. & Eleanor J. Andersen Foundation; the David & Mary Anderson Family Foundation; the Buuck Family Foundation; the Dorsey & Whitney Foundation; Dorsey & Whitney LLP; Fredrikson & Byron, P.A.; the Fringe Foundation; Kenneth Koch Literary Estate; the Knight Foundation; the Rehael Fund of the Minneapolis Foundation; the Matching Grant Program Fund of the Minneapolis Foundation; Mr. Pancks' Fund in memory of Graham Kimpton; the Schwab Charitable Fund; Schwegman, Lundberg & Woessner, P.A.; the US Bank Foundation; VSA Minnesota for the Metropolitan Regional Arts Council; and the Woessner Freeman Family Foundation in honor of Allan Kornblum.

The Publisher's Circle of Coffee House Press

Publisher's Circle members make significant contributions to Coffee House Press's annual giving campaign. Understanding that a strong financial base is necessary for the press to meet the challenges and opportunities that arise each year, this group plays a crucial part in the success of Coffee House's mission.

Recent Publisher's Circle members include many anonymous donors, Suzanne Allen, Patricia A. Beithon, Bill Berkson & Connie Lewallen, E. Thomas Binger & Rebecca Rand Fund of the Minneapolis Foundation, Robert & Gail Buuck, Claire Casey, Louise Copeland, Jane Dalrymple-Hollo, Ruth Stricker Dayton, Jennifer Kwon Dobbs & Stefan Liess, Mary Ebert & Paul Stembler, Sally French, Chris Fischbach & Katie Dublinski, Kaywin Feldman & Jim Lutz, Sally French, Jocelyn Hale & Glenn Miller, the Rehael Fund-Roger Hale/Nor Hall of the Minneapolis Foundation, Randy Hartten & Ron Lotz, Dylan Hicks & Nina Hale, Jeffrey Hom, Carl & Heidi Horsch, Amy L. Hubbard & Geoffrey J. Kehoe Fund, Kenneth Kahn & Susan Dicker, Stephen & Isabel Keating, Kenneth Koch Literary Estate, Allan & Cinda Kornblum, Leslie Larson Maheras, Lenfestey Family Foundation, Sarah Lutman & Rob Rudolph, the Carol & Aaron Mack Charitable Fund of the Minneapolis Foundation, George & Olga Mack, Joshua Mack & Ron Warren, Gillian McCain, Mary & Malcolm McDermid, Sjur Midness & Briar Andresen, Maureen Millea Smith & Daniel Smith, Peter Nelson & Jennifer Swenson, Marc Porter & James Hennessy, Enrique Olivarez, Jr. & Jennifer Komar, Alan Polsky, Robin Preble, Jeffrey Scherer, Jeffrey Sugerman & Sarah Schultz, Alexis Scott, Nan G. & Stephen C. Swid, Patricia Tilton, Stu Wilson & Melissa Barker, Warren D. Woessner & Iris C. Freeman, Margaret Wurtele, Joanne Von Blon, and Wayne P. Zink & Christopher Schout.

For more information about the Publisher's Circle and other ways
to support Coffee House Press books, authors, and activities,
please visit www.coffeehousepress.org/support or
contact us at info@coffeehousepress.org.

Also by Victor Hernández Cruz

 *In the Shadow of Al-Andalus*

 *Maraca*

 *The Mountain in the Sea*

 *Panoramas*

 *Red Beans*

Beneath the Spanish was typeset by
Bookmobile Design & Digital Publisher Services.
Text is set in Sabon.